How to
Write a
Better Thesis

If it's not written, it's not research.

How to Write a Better Thesis

David Evans and Paul Gruba

Second edition

MELBOURNE
UNIVERSITY
PRESS

MELBOURNE UNIVERSITY PRESS
An imprint of Melbourne University Publishing Ltd
187 Gratton Street, Carlton, Victoria 3053, Australia
mup-info@unimelb.edu.au
www.mup.com.au

First published 2002
Reprinted 2004 (twice), 2005, 2007
Text © David Evans and Paul Gruba 2002

Design and typography © Melbourne University Press 2002

Designed by Jan Schmoeger/Designpoint
Typeset in 10.5/14 point ITC New Baskerville
by Syarikat Seng Teik Sdn. Bhd., Malaysia
Printed in Australia by McPherson's Printing Group

National Library of Australia Cataloguing-in-Publication entry

Evans, D. G. (David G.).
   How to write a better thesis.

   2nd ed.
   Bibliography.
   Includes index.
   ISBN 978 0 522 85030 7.

   1. Report writing. 2. Dissertations, Academic. I. Gruba,
Paul. II. Title.

808.02

Contents

Preface to the second edition

This book was first published in 1995, and has been reprinted nearly every year since. Judging by the letters and emails I have received from all over Australia and from overseas it seems to have filled a need. But it was starting to show its age.

In the original book I made a strong point of using the word processor to prepare theses, emphasizing that it opened up a new way of approaching the research task. The old idea of deferring the writing until the research was finished could now be abandoned, and the two tasks could proceed side by side. Since then there has been a revolution in the use of word processors, and undergraduates now do most of their assignments with them. It was time for a rewrite.

In preparing this second edition, I asked Paul Gruba to join me as co-author. Paul teaches in the University of Melbourne's Centre for Communication Skills and English as a Second Language. His experience complements mine. Mine has bridged the physical and social sciences; his has bridged the social sciences and the humanities. Whereas I have been supervising theses for nearly forty years, Paul has only recently completed his own PhD. He brings some fresh insights to the process of writing a thesis—he has faced the same issues that many of you currently face. For several years he has been using my book as a resource for courses in thesis writing, and has found by experience what was useful and what was not. Many of his critical comments about the shortcomings of the original book have been taken into account in this second edition.

What changes have we made in this book? Most of the advice I gave in the original edition has stood the test of time. Indeed, much of what I was tentatively feeling towards has been confirmed by work with another batch of PhD students. Although most of the ideas would be useful for people writing reports, we have in this edition limited the scope to thesis writing. This has permitted us to write a new chapter on what a thesis is all about. Our starting point for this was the procedures used at the University of Melbourne, not because they are superior to those used elsewhere but because we are familiar with them. We have also sharpened the focus on how to disseminate material from your own project. Technical information has been updated, and key ideas summarized and highlighted.

There are, of course, many ways of writing a thesis, and particular universities and disciplines might have approaches that differ from what we are recommending. Guides and handbooks from a number of disciplines are listed in the Bibliography. You should treat what we have to say as a general guide, embodying ideas that we have found useful in our university, and in the disciplines that we are most familiar with, and not try to follow them slavishly.

Many students over the past few years have told me that one of the features of the book that gave it an edge of believability was its conversational style. This was readily achieved when I wrote alone, but presented some difficulties with the two of us working collaboratively. We have tried to deal with this problem by using the word 'we' when we are giving you advice jointly, but using the word 'I' when clearly only one of us was speaking, for example the anecdotes used to illustrate certain points. We have kept most of these anecdotes and have added a few more, some from Paul's experience. Paul's carry his name. The rest are from my experience.

Many people have helped us to make this second edition, I hope, better than the original. We thank the students who have used the book to assist them in writing their theses, and those who have taken part in thesis-writing short courses at the University of Melbourne under our guidance. Their comments and reactions have given us many insights into what worked and what didn't. Our special thanks go to Gillian Fulcher, our editor, for her care in reading the manuscript. She gently insisted that we clarify obscure passages, and made many valuable suggestions.

David Evans

1 Introduction

One of the examiners of Joe's thesis rang me to say that it 'read like a novel'. Looking back, I don't think this was a particularly apt simile, as a novel has a different purpose and requires different skills, but I certainly knew what he meant. The story developed surely and clearly; Joe always knew where he was going; and at the end it was completely clear what he had achieved, what his conclusions were, and how they responded to the aim he had announced at the beginning of the thesis. Needless to say he passed, without any fuss.

The skills required to report the results of research or investigations are more straightforward than those of the novelist. At least they *should* be, because thesis writers have a very straightforward task: to convey to the reader in a convincing way what they have found out. In practice it is rather more difficult. Of the forty or so higher-degree candidates we have supervised over the years, only one or two had the gift of getting it all down with ease, and with little criticism. Most of them needed this criticism and got it, and produced theses that the examiners passed. Our aim in this book is to write down what we have learnt from our experiences of trying to help students produce theses that examiners find acceptable.

Chapters 2 to 4 show you how to get started, and what decisions to make before you start. Chapters 5 to 11 show you how to tackle the various parts of a thesis and bring it to the point of submission. You will wish to report work in progress in seminars and conferences, and the final outcomes of your project as papers in learned journals (you will, truly). Chapter 12 deals with the modifications in approach required for seminars and papers because of their differences in scope, purpose, readership and length. It also suggests some ways of dealing with the tricky problem of joint authorship, with colleagues or your supervisor.

We have both used the first edition of the book as a source book for seminars and workshops on thesis writing. Those who are well into their writing seem to get immediate benefit from the ideas in it. However, if you are at an early stage, we suggest you first read Chapters 2 and 3. When you get to Chapter 4, which introduces you to the power of the word processor, you will probably find that there are more ideas in it than you can absorb straight away. Some of it may not take on an edge of reality until you are well into your writing. Don't be discouraged: we can assure you that everything in this chapter is very important in the writing of a good thesis. So, please take our advice and try to use the word processor creatively, right from the start. Read through Chapter 4 now to get some sense of all the things that the word processor can help you with, and at least learn how to use a thesis template. You will then be ready to step off on the right foot, and you will come back to this chapter later to learn more of what it can do for you.

2 What's a thesis?

Thomas was walking around the corridor outside my (Paul Gruba's) office, wondering out loud, 'I don't even know what a thesis is, so how can I get started?' He had spent most of the morning talking with his supervisor, and she had told him that a thesis was essentially an extended academic argument. She was right, but Thomas was frustrated with her answer. He wanted more detail, more guidance and a better understanding of the type of document he would need to produce over the next three years.

Criteria for examination

After reading many theses, the regulations that surround their submission, and many examiners' reports, we've come to the conclusion that there is no clear definition of a thesis. It seems that everyone does things differently, that different fields follow different conventions, and that different supervisors, and indeed different examiners, have their own ideas on what constitutes a thesis. So, rather than looking for a specific definition, we suggest that you take a look at what examiners are required to report on. When universities send out a thesis for examination, they enclose a copy of their guidelines for examiners. The first thing you need to do, then, is to get a copy of these guidelines from your own university and look them over carefully. What do they suggest examiners should look for? Once you know how and on what principles you will be examined, you will have a better understanding of what is required to make a thesis. And, hopefully, you will come to see what a thesis is.

At our university, the guidelines begin by listing key attributes of a successful thesis (see Box 1).*

- The thesis demonstrates authority in the candidate's field and shows evidence of command of knowledge in relevant fields.
- It shows that the candidate has a thorough grasp of the appropriate methodological techniques and an awareness of their limitations.
- It makes a distinct contribution to knowledge.
- Its contribution to knowledge rests on originality of approach and/or interpretation of the findings and, in some cases, the discovery of new facts.
- It demonstrates an ability to communicate research findings effectively in the professional arena and in an international context.
- It is a careful, rigorous and sustained piece of work demonstrating that a research 'apprenticeship' is complete and the holder is admitted to the community of scholars in the discipline.

Box 1: Attributes of a thesis needed to pass an examination

Although these guidelines seem at first to refer to the thesis, they are really about the candidate. The first point makes this quite explicit: 'The thesis demonstrates authority in the candidate's field . . .' And look at the last point. The examiner has to

---

* The text in Boxes 1 and 2 is quoted from *The Degree of Doctor of Philosophy Handbook*, School of Graduate Studies, University of Melbourne, 2000.

consider whether 'it [the thesis] is a careful, rigorous and sustained piece of work'—but look how it goes on—'demonstrating that a research "apprenticeship" is complete and the holder [you hopefully] is [can be?] admitted to the community of scholars in the discipline'.

When we ask students in introductory seminars what they think the purpose of a thesis is their reply is usually something along the lines, 'To tell people in my area what I have found out'. No doubt some people in your field will look carefully at your thesis in the years to come, but your main readership is the examiners. And the examiners are not reading your work to discover what you have found out. No, it is clear from the guidelines that they are reading it to see whether you should be admitted to the international community of scholars in your field—the thesis is primarily an examination paper, not a report of your findings. (That will be reserved for the papers you will write as a result of your research—see Chapter 12.) Throughout this book we will often refer to what the examiners are looking for.

Let us turn now to the set of questions that accompany the guidelines for thesis examiners. In the case of doctoral theses, they are asked to consider eight questions (see Box 2).

These questions really are about the thesis rather than the candidate. They roughly parallel the structure of a good, solid thesis. Each one builds on the previous one. Questions 1 and 2 are about familiarity with the previous work in your field and the demonstration of a critical approach to it. (We will discuss how to review previous work critically in Chapter 6.) Having read what others have said and done, you are now ready to do some work yourself. Question 3 is about choosing appropriate research methods *and* saying why you chose them (see Chapter 7). Question 4 is about applying the methods, getting the results and making sense of them (see Chapter 8). Questions 5 and 6 are about interpreting your results in such a way as to achieve your original aim (see Chapters 9 and 10). You will notice the emphasis on linking your interpretations back to what you said you would do earlier in the thesis.

---

1 Does the candidate show sufficient familiarity with, and understanding and critical appraisal of, the relevant literature?

2 Does the thesis provide a sufficiently comprehensive investigation of the topic?

3 Are the methods and techniques adopted appropriate to the subject matter and are they properly justified and applied?

4 Are the results suitably set out and accompanied by adequate exposition and interpretation?

5 Are conclusions and implications appropriately developed and clearly linked to the nature and content of the research framework and findings?

6 Has the research question(s) in fact been tested?

7 Is the literary quality and general presentation of the thesis of a suitably high standard?

8 Does the thesis as a whole constitute a substantive original contribution to knowledge in the subject area with which it deals?

Box 2: Key questions for examining a PhD thesis

Finally, Questions 7 and 8 don't relate to the structure of the thesis, but to the quality of the work as a whole. Much of the material in Chapter 4 is about how to make a high quality presentation. Chapter 11 doesn't guarantee that you will make 'a substantive original contribution to knowledge', but it does take you through a checklist to ensure that you have done everything properly, and that the argument in the thesis flows logically (in future, we refer to this as logic flow).

Looking at other theses

It's now time to look at some sample theses. Most supervisors will have a few on their shelves that they will be willing to lend you. This will be a good start, but you shouldn't stop there. The theses your supervisor lends you will most likely follow a pattern set by your supervisor's own ideas of a good thesis, and almost certainly they will be typical of what your own department thinks is acceptable. So go out and look at theses from across a range of disciplines, and even theses from other countries.* As methods of presentation have been advancing rapidly in the last few years (see Chapter 4), try to find theses no more than three years old. If applicable, examine a mix of quantitative and qualitative studies. After you have skimmed through some you have found, select one that seems to be coherent, and one that is not so clear, and ask your supervisor to go through them with you.

First, with the Guidelines for Examiners in front of you look at the overall layout. See if the table of contents gives you a clear idea of the structure of the work as a whole. Then skim over the introduction, move to the conclusions and flip through the reference section. You will find how easy it is to read someone else's thesis as if you were the examiner, and get an overall feel for the level of professionalism it displays. Next, read the introduction carefully and flip to the conclusions to see if the work is linked together in a coherent manner (see Question 5 in Box 2). It might surprise you to find that some theses fail to make this link. Resolve to avoid the mistakes that others have made.

You might also be impressed with some of the virtues of these other theses, for example good layouts, innovative ways to display complex material in graphs or tables, or a strong integration of online materials. Stay alert for the points that impress you, and make a note to adapt them for your own work.

---

* A number of Australian and overseas theses are available online at
<http://www.ndltd.org/members/index.htm>

SUMMARY

- There is no readily available 'standard' definition of a thesis. The expectations for the work vary from university to university, from field to field and even from supervisor to supervisor.
- Understand your university's criteria for examining theses, and be sure to craft your own work so that it meets these criteria.
- Look over a variety of theses from your own field and across a variety of disciplines.
- Pretend you are an examiner and read these other theses critically. Note points that you wish to avoid, and those that might be adapted for your own work.

3 Making a strong start

Len had completed an experimental program in an area of engineering and was now ready to write his thesis, but he was having trouble starting. He had been reading the literature on his topic ever since he had been enrolled, and was by now very knowledgeable in the field. He decided that the first thing he had to write was a review of this literature (more of this in Chapter 6). I told him that I would like to see an outline of how he expected to tackle it in one week's time. Two weeks later nothing had appeared. I went to see him, and asked what the problem was. 'No problem', he replied, 'It's just that I still have seven more papers to read. When I've read them I'll start writing.' I reminded him that he'd told me two weeks ago that he had only two more papers to read, and then he would start writing. He explained that, while reading one of these two, he'd turned up several more papers. He then showed me a little metal card box containing a card for every paper he'd read, with its details and his abstract of what it was saying. (This was in the days before computers and Endnote®, which is an electronic way of doing the same thing.) I asked him how many cards were in it. 'A hundred and twenty, with seven more to come.' He was never going to start. He told himself that finding new papers was the reason, but it was clear that the problem lay deeper.

Why we have trouble starting

Research is not a completely rational process. In nearly every research project I have been connected with, the conclusions contained some quite unexpected elements. In most projects the aim of the work changed during the course of it, sometimes several times. Often I've had students come to me and say that their 'experiments had failed', but when we had absorbed the implications of the supposed failure new hypotheses emerged that resulted in breakthroughs in their research. On several occasions quite remarkable conclusions were staring the student (and me) in the face, yet we failed to see them for weeks or even months because we were so hooked on what we *expected* to find out.

In the classical application of the 'scientific method' the researcher is supposed to develop a hypothesis, then design a crucial experiment to test it. If the hypothesis withstands this test a generalization is then argued for, and an advance in understanding has been made. But where did the hypothesis come from in the first place? I have a colleague whose favourite question is 'Why is this so?' and I've seen this innocent question spawn brilliant research projects on quite a few occasions. Thus, research is a peculiar mixture of creative thinking (hypothesis generation, musing over the odd and surprising), and rational thinking (design and execution of crucial experiments, analysis of results in terms of existing theory). Most of the books on research methods and design of experiments (you will find hundreds of them in your university library) are concerned with the rational part, and fail to deal with the creative part. Yet without the creative part no real research would ever be done, no new insights would ever be gained, and no new theories would ever be formulated.

A thesis is, of course, an account of the outcome of this rational/creative research process, and writing it is also a rational/creative process. However, the emphasis is far more on the rational side than the creative side—we have to convince the examiners with our arguments. Yet all of us know that we do write creatively, at least in the fine detail of it. We talk of our pens (or fingers on the keyboard) running ahead of our brains, as if our fingers were the creative bit of us and our brains the rational bit. This is, of course, nonsense, and we know it, yet the experience is there.

Wrestling with this problem has led me to the view that all writing, like all research, involves the tension between the creative and the rational parts of our brains. It is this tension that makes it so hard for us to start writing, that sometimes gives us 'writer's block'. To get started, we must resolve the tension. In this chapter we shall describe some ways for doing this.

Thinking rationally about your thesis

My colleague Bill was worried about the draft thesis that had been submitted to him by Henry, one of his students, and asked me to look at it. It was certainly very difficult to know what was going on. Henry had written it straight from his log book, experiment after experiment, in chronological order:

> *Experiment No. 37*: as Experiment 36 failed to show the chemical reaction I expected, I next tried the effect of doubling the concentration of the active reagent . . .

and so on. Your task as writer is to make the outcome comprehensible to the readers, not to take them along all the highways and byways and down the cul-de-sacs that you entered while establishing this outcome. It is essential that you structure your thesis in such a way that you take the reader from the aim to the conclusions in the clearest possible way, and by the most direct route.

11

As we noted in the last chapter, there is no such thing as a standard thesis. However, our examination of the guidelines for thesis examiners did suggest a standard thesis *structure*. This structure is outlined in Figure 1. Our experience is that it works well for theses in the physical, biological and social sciences and, with some minor variations in style of reporting, for the humanities.

We shall discuss other possible structures separately after we have looked at the 'standard' thesis structure.

The 'standard' thesis structure

The standard thesis structure consists of four parts (see Figure 1). Some of these parts might contain more than one chapter. The arrows show the logic flow between the parts.

* Part 1 is the introduction. Don't mess around in it. Quite literally, the only purpose it has is to introduce the research. You should start by outlining the problem you intend to investigate, state the aim of the research, limit the scope of your investigation and then provide an overview of what lies ahead. Three to five pages are enough for this.
* Part 2 is the background required before you can describe your own research. In this section, your purpose is to position your study in the context of what has gone before, what is currently taking place and how research in the area is conducted. To start, it might contain a brief historical review. If the research is location-specific you will need a chapter or chapters describing the study area and its characteristics. It will usually contain a chapter reviewing current theory or practice. You might include the results of preliminary experiments or surveys carried out to help you feel your way into the problem.
* Part 3 will concern your own work. It will contain the design of experiments, surveys or reviews to test hypotheses or answer questions developed from the background chapters. Next come the results of this work, and analysis of the results.

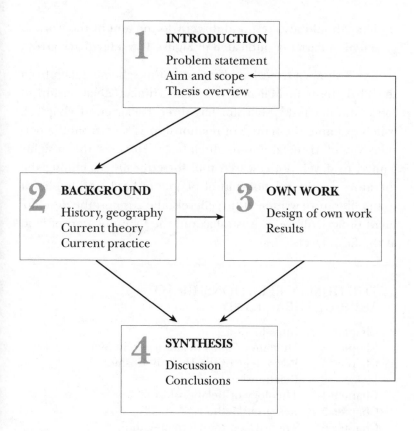

Figure 1: Structure of theses in the physical, biological and social sciences

- Part 4, the synthesis, develops your own contribution to the state of knowledge and understanding of the topic. It will usually contain a discussion in which you examine your own results in the light of the previous state of the subject as outlined in Part 2. This may lead to the development of new theory. If you have been building a model it will contain an evaluation of the model, to see whether it does what you hoped it would do. Finally, you will draw this discussion or evaluation together to produce conclusions. These should, of course, arise directly out of the discussion or evaluation.

They should also respond directly to the aim of the work as stated in Part 1, as indicated in Figure 1 by a feedback arrow.

Box 3 shows a typical application of this scheme, taken from the PhD thesis of Malcolm Ives, The Human Relationship to Agricultural Land.* Malcolm has three background chapters, which examine the nature of relationship as seen from the perspectives of three different disciplines. He uses the insights gained to develop a research tool for critically examining the literature on the relationship of people to land, and applies it to the literature written at three levels: the cosmos; the development of agriculture in Australia; and the manipulation of land at the farm level.

THE HUMAN RELATIONSHIP TO AGRICULTURAL LAND

Chapter 1	Introduction
Chapter 2	Human–Cosmos Relationship in Myth
Chapter 3	Psychology of the Human–Cosmos Relationship
Chapter 4	Theology of Relationship
Chapter 5	Research Method
Chapter 6	Theories on the Human–Land Relationship
Chapter 7	Symbolism in Agriculture in Australia
Chapter 8	Soil Conservation and Keyline Farming
Chapter 9	Discussion
Chapter 10	Conclusions

Box 3: Content outline of a thesis using the standard structure

If you stick to this four-part structure you will write a clear and comprehensible thesis. We will deal with these four parts in detail in Chapters 5 to 10. Our purpose in this chapter is to convince

---

* All theses and research reports referred to are listed separately in the Bibliography.

you that you should neglect none of these four sections, and that you should develop them in the order given in Figure 1. If you neglect any of them you will get into strife. For example, in the seminars we have held for 'Getting your thesis started' over the past few years students have often told us that their supervisors insist that the introductory chapter should consist of a survey of the literature describing what others had previously done in the area, ending up by deducing some hypotheses to help in the design of their own work. This amounts to eliminating Part 1 of our diagram altogether, and starting the thesis at Part 2. The danger is that the reader will get lost in the detail of the literature, and never find out what the project is trying to do. What's worse, without this introductory chapter you may never really identify the purpose of your investigation yourself.

How many chapters should there be? If there are four main parts, each containing one to three chapters, we should not expect more than eight or ten chapters. Many theses are accomplished in five to seven chapters. If you have more than ten, you should suspect that some are really only sections of chapters, and you should attempt some consolidation. My university once asked me to report on a request for financial assistance to publish a thesis as a book. It had around thirty chapters! The simple and coherent structure shown in Figure 1 was totally obscured by the proliferation of chapters with seemingly arbitrary titles. The effect of this was total disintegration, and I was surprised that the examiners had passed it.

Reportage and structure

Look for the structure behind your reportage, and don't confuse reportage with structure. Reportage is the way structure is written up. The nature of research in the humanities is different from that in the sciences,[*] and different forms of reportage may be

---

[*] C. Belsey, *Critical Practice.*

appropriate for theses in this area. For example, in the second edition of their book *Thesis and Assignment Writing* J. Anderson and M. Poole give a checklist for organizing theses based on empirical or experimental studies, and another for theses of an analytical or literary kind. We paraphrase their checklists in Figure 2. Despite the different procedures used, the structures of the two types of thesis are quite similar.

Thesis on Empirical/Experimental Study	Thesis on Analytical/Literary Study
Problem	**Objective**
The problem	Purpose of the study
Significance of the problem	Contribution of the study to knowledge
Relationship to previous work	Evaluation of previous studies
Derivation of hypotheses	
Procedures	**Procedures**
Design of own experiments or work	Assumptions
Results of own work	Sources
	Documentation
Analysis	**Analysis**
Analysis of results	Analysis of facts
	Evaluation of material
Conclusions	**Conclusions**

Figure 2: Forms of reportage in theses for the sciences and the humanities.

SOURCE: Adapted from Anderson and Poole, *Thesis and Assignment Writing*, 2nd edn pp. 143–5.

Non-standard thesis structures

A number of theses, of course, do not fit into a standard structure. In some disciplines, there appears to be more of a blending of quantitative and qualitative approaches. Such work, for example, might include an indepth examination of the context and history of a situation before it arrives at a 'statement of the problem'. A quantitative survey might inform the development of interview questions, and these in turn might lead to a circular analysis of the results that, again, may suggest yet another series of questions. A conceptual framework may be an outcome and not a starting point.

If you are writing a thesis that relies on a non-standard structure, it is a good idea to read completed theses that have also taken such a tack. Immerse yourself, too, in a number of handbooks that help with the writing up of qualitative research, and be sure that you establish a clear line of argumentation throughout your work.* Too often qualitative researchers run the risk of merely describing their complex settings and ignore the need to demonstrate critical thinking.

Be sure that you know the criteria for examination. Although you may be doing something 'different', this does not absolve you from creating a strong academic argument underpinned by sound evidence, credible analysis and clear writing. In qualitative work, for example, you will need to examine the many challenges that surround qualitative data collection and analysis. And the data you collect will need to be presented in such a way that it develops into a clear conceptual framework.

Writing modes

PhD applicants at the University of Melbourne are first admitted to probationary candidature. If they are studying full-time, at the end of their first nine months they are asked to prepare a confirmation report for submission by the end of their first year. A Confirmation Committee has to examine this report and satisfy itself that the candidate has a viable project and is on the right track to earn a doctorate. If they are satisfied, the applicant will be admitted to full candidature. What is needed in this report to satisfy the Committee? The left-hand column

---

* A good account of writing up qualitative research can be found in M. B. Miles and A. M. Huberman, *Qualitative Data Analysis: An Expanded Sourcebook*.

in Figure 3 shows points that should be considered. In the right-hand column, we compare these with a draft of the 'standard' thesis structure.

Confirmation Report	Draft Thesis
Title of thesis	Preliminary pages
Description of research project	
Introduction	Chapter 1 Introduction
Overview of relevant research	Chapters 2, 3 Background chapters
Questions raised by this overview	Chapter 4 Research Design
Proposed research procedure	
Research methods	Chapter 4 Research Design
Data sources and data collection	Chapter 4 Research Design
Research timetable	
Bibliography	

Figure 3: Contents of confirmation report—what you should have done in the first year

You will notice the similarities between the two columns. Clearly, the University of Melbourne expects that after one year of full-time study PhD candidates are able to write a draft introduction chapter containing a problem statement, an aim and an outline of the thesis. Draft background chapters, and a draft research design chapter are also expected. At this point, they also expect that you have read enough to produce a reasonable bibliography. Moreover, you need to be organized well enough to say how you are going to complete your research and write and submit your thesis in the next two years. A bit daunting! Yet if you don't get this far in the first year, our experience is that you won't finish in three years. How are you going to do it?

Write early and often

Let us describe a typical first six months of a PhD or research masters project. If you are working on a topic nominated by your department, it is likely that your supervisor has set you some reading to do to catch up with what your predecessors have done. Following this reading you will be asked to write a review showing how the field has been developing and, hopefully, what problems still remain. Alternatively you may have chosen a topic yourself. In this case your supervisor will ask you to describe the topic, and will ask you why it is worth spending three years of your life on. After some discussion, no doubt you will again be set the task of reading the literature on one or more topics relevant to your chosen topic and writing reviews of them.

In either case, your first piece of research will be a review of existing work in the area. You may be tempted to write this as a 'data dump', a compendium of abstracts of all the papers you have read. We hope you don't do this! A slightly more constructive approach would be to write this as a chronology of how the topic has developed. Or, perhaps better still, you could write it as an encyclopedic review. Neither of these will take you beyond the present 'state of the art' in your topic, but they should get you thinking more deeply about it. No doubt as your supervisor reads your draft reviews you will be criticized for your omissions, your neglect of important ideas or your superficiality. But you will be making progress.

As this initial reviewing work develops you should be able to define your topic more carefully, and put some limits around it. You will gradually find out what the real unanswered questions are. You may be able to reformulate these as hypotheses. And you might be able to devise a tentative method or methods for answering your questions or testing your hypotheses. Soon you could write a thesis structure—a tentative Table of Contents— like those discussed earlier in this chapter, for example the one given in Box 3. If you are in the University of Melbourne you could write a persuasive account of all of this and have your candidacy confirmed.

Without realizing it, you have not only started your research but you have started writing your thesis. You could then start to force some of those earlier pieces your supervisor asked you to write into chapters in the thesis mould (we shall talk about this later in the chapter). When research and writing go on simultaneously, there are three potential benefits. We have hinted at the first of them above: arguing out your ideas in writing will help you to think more constructively about them. It will help you to identify the processes that enabled you to reach these insights, and you will know that you will have to bring them out in your reviews of existing theory or practice. All of this should lead to sharper research questions or hypotheses, and better design of your research program. The second benefit is that if you start to write at an early stage you will be well into your writing before you have done your own surveys or experiments. Therefore, unlike Len, you will not be faced with the formidable task of 'getting started' on your writing when you have all but finished your research, because you will have started long ago. You will be getting valuable feedback on your ideas and writing throughout your candidature. The third benefit is that it will help you to give shape to your project, including the thesis that reports on it, at an early stage. To explain this, we shall now outline how you might go about it.[*]

We described earlier in the chapter the standard structure for a thesis. You will have seen from the above account of preparing a confirmation report that you could devise this structure at a very early stage of the work. To do this, first write a draft of your introductory chapter—the problem statement, the aim and scope, and the steps you think you might take to achieve the aim. You may not feel too confident about writing this introduction, because you suspect that it will have to be modified later, as you get into your work. In this you are almost certainly correct, but that should not prevent you from writing a *draft* introduction. What you are trying to do is 'get started'.

[*] This method, and the example on ecotourism that we will use shortly, owe a lot to my former colleague Laurie Cosgrove. I jointly supervised some projects with her using it. It works.

As an example, suppose you decide to do some research on ecotourism. Your supervisor, no doubt, will ask what the aim of your research is. Probably you will have trouble with this question, as you became interested in ecotourism only because you suspected that there were some inherent problems in the idea. However, as a way of proceeding, you settle on the following tentative aim for your project: 'To establish whether ecotourism will help to preserve ecological systems'. Starting to write will help you to clarify this aim, and eventually help you define the scope of the study.

You will see straight away how difficult it is to write a critical review of the literature on ecotourism at this early stage. But what you can do quite easily is review the appropriate background. There are some things that you will need to be familiar with to achieve your aim:

- Definitions of ecotourism
- History of ecotourism: Where did the idea come from? What has happened since?
- What are the problems with ecotourism? (This would be an expansion of your problem statement.)
- What has been the response to date from tour operators and from governments?

When you have read the literature and written a piece on each of these you will be far better informed about your project, and may have revised your aim. You will have a better idea of how you might limit your study. You will certainly be in a much better position to devise surveys of potential ecotourists, and interviews with tour operators. The writing will not be wasted. You will incorporate much of it in your final thesis, although you will no doubt make many changes before that.

Thinking your way into your project like this will help you to write a tentative structure for the first part of your thesis. Of course, you will have a big blank in the last two chapters, which will just read 'Discussion' and 'Conclusions'. But you now have enough to draw up a tentative table of contents.

Next, get a loose-leaf folder, with a set of card dividers. Paste the structures for each chapter on individual card dividers. Insert the draft table of contents for the whole report in the front. Then decide which chapter or section of a chapter you could tackle first, and start writing. (As you can see from the ecotourism example, it is better at this stage to write a 'factual' chapter first, rather than attempt one where you will be forced to make many interpretations or judgements. A strong understanding of the literature will help you identify the key areas of this field and thus focus your study.) As you write you should try to follow the 'rational' structure you have predetermined. But once you start writing to this 'rational' outline you should let your fingers do the talking: slip uninhibitedly into creative-writing mode. When you have written the chapter, insert it behind the appropriate card divider as the first version of that chapter. If it is not a complete chapter, write a few notes on the missing sections to indicate how you envisage that you will construct the whole chapter, and how the material you have written fits in. Every time you go to a meeting with your supervisor or supervisors, take the folder with you. *It is the latest draft of your thesis.*

As a result of your own work and thinking, and your discussions on the progress of the project with your supervisors and others, you will no doubt see many gaps and inconsistencies in your draft structure. Revise the structure to deal with these problems whenever necessary, drawing up a new table of contents and new chapter structures and introductions, and sort your folder into the new structure. You will retain some of the material you wrote previously, although you might put it in different chapters. For the time being, put any material for which you cannot find a home in an appendix at the back, labelled with a title (you will probably reject it eventually, but it might be useful later). As results start to emerge from your own work, they will take their place quite easily as one or more 'Results' chapters. Then you will have many ideas and even arguments about what they signify, and drafts of the 'Discussion' and 'Conclusions' chapters will start to emerge (we shall discuss a process for getting these into shape in Chapters 9 and 10). These drafts will also be tucked behind the appropriate card dividers. One day you will walk into a meeting with your supervisors, and you will all realize that the thesis has taken its final shape—all it needs is the final working through to turn it into the first draft of the complete work. We hope we have made it sound easy. If you do it this way, it is.

Writing up at the end

I mentioned earlier Len's problem in starting to write his thesis. When he wrote his thesis over twenty years ago, word processors had not been invented, and the integrated research/writing process that we have just discussed was hardly possible. Instead, we had the 'research first and write later' model of thesis writing.

Despite the flexibility now offered by the word processor, it seems that old habits die hard amongst supervisors. Judging from the seminars we have held on 'Starting your thesis', many supervisors, especially in the experimental sciences, are still advocating the old method, and some even discourage their students from writing until they have finished their main experiments. If you do this, you are in danger of writing your thesis around the results of these experiments, and neglecting to tell the reader of the many steps that have gone into obtaining these results. As an examiner, I am never impressed by a thesis that gives an account of ingenious experiments and the results obtained from them, but fails to tell me why the experiments were carried out or what the implications of the findings were.

I did manage to get Len going eventually. This is how I did it: I asked him how many important ideas he had identified in those 120 papers, ideas that had taken the theory of his topic along another step. To my surprise, he replied almost immediately that there were only four, and explained them. I saw that somehow his unconscious mind had been working on those 120 papers, sorting them, organizing them, ordering them. I could see that these four ideas would doubtless provide the titles of four sections of his review of existing theory, and suggested he start writing on this basis. He came back in two weeks with a brilliant review of the theory that scarcely needed any change.

My advice to Len enabled him to get started because it gave him a structure to write to. I think we were a bit lucky, as the review of existing theory is not an easy chapter to start on. Nevertheless, it did work, because it enabled him to resolve the tension between his rational, conscious thinking and his creative, unconscious thinking. To get started on the thesis at this late stage you must acknowledge and *harness* this tension. To do this you must first devise a logical structure for the whole thesis, using the general format outlined earlier in this chapter (see Figure 1). A good way to ensure that the structure is sound is to write the introductions to each chapter, then string them together to see whether the report develops logically. The tentative table of contents (chapter headings and section headings within chapters) should reflect this logic. Then, start to write.

When we were describing the early-start model of thesis writing we suggested that students begin by writing the introductory chapter that described why they were doing the research, what their aim and scope were, and how they intended to achieve their aim. This advice holds for the late-start model also. If you are having trouble with this chapter, you most likely have not yet got the aim of the whole project right. (Yes, this can happen even after you have completed all your surveys or experimental work!) Put this chapter aside for the moment, and start with another. As we mentioned above, a good idea is to start with a factual chapter, one describing the study area, or the rationale for selecting a research method, or the design of experiments or questionnaires. These are chapters in which the rational side of writing will predominate, and the creative side will not provide a stumbling block.*

Again, follow the structure that you have devised with the rational side of your brain but, once you start the writing itself, allow the creative side of your brain to work through the argument for you. When you have finished writing for the day, save what you have written. Then go to bed, and sleep on it (the very existence of this expression is evidence that our unconscious thinking processes keep working even when all rational thinking has been switched off). Your first task the next day is to look at the chapter outline, then read, on the screen, the chapter as it stands. As well as picking up typographical and grammatical errors you will readily see the results of the tension between creative writing and rational structure. If you find that they are at odds, one of them must give. Either your original rational structure was wrong, in which case you must alter it, or your creative thinking has taken you on a wild-goose chase, in which case you must cut the errant material out. But you now have inputs from both sides of your brain, and can sit in judgement on the outcome.

Very soon you will find that you have written a chapter, or at least some sections of one. You have started! You, like Len, will have no problem in continuing with the process of writing, gradually building up a complete thesis.

Starting, and starting again

Other students seem to have a problem that is the opposite of Len's. They start an introduction, look at it, and then start writing

---

* It is not a good idea to start with a 'critical review' of existing theory, as used to be fashionable, indeed compulsory. How one could be 'critical' in these circumstances is quite beyond us. This is probably the hardest chapter for an inexperienced student to write, as it demands a strong resolution of the tension between the creative and rational sides of writing. (In fact, as we discuss in Chapter 6, we don't believe one should have a chapter headed 'Literature Review' in a thesis, anyway.)

another introduction! They get caught in a seemingly endless cycle of starting and re-starting, each time thinking that they must get this right before they can do anything. It is at this point they often come for help.

Kevin was one such student: he came to my (Paul Gruba's) office with three different starts. After looking at his first introduction, I gave him some advice about improving it, and he went away to write another. In his second version, however, he had decided to alter the direction of his thesis and had changed tack. Here, he omitted parts, saved some and expanded others. It still wasn't quite right. This happened three times. With each re-write, he emphasized different points that suggested different areas of investigations. His co-supervisor, like me, would get frustrated and call me: it appeared to her that Kevin didn't really know what he wanted to do with his own study. Was he good enough to finish a thesis if he couldn't start? In his defence, Kevin said that he was trying to cover all his bases and explore several lines of enquiry so that he wouldn't get caught out further down the track. He wanted to be certain that he would pass without any major glitches.

It is crucial at this point that you try to make yourself stick to something: it may not be perfect, but you need to get started. You need to pursue one line of reasoning before you change to another. This is particularly true if you are undertaking a Masters or Honours thesis: you have a very limited word count and a tight deadline to meet. I knew that Kevin had read a great deal of literature, and so I asked him to list the key areas he was interested in. What, I asked, was interesting enough to pursue in the coming years? Within a short time, he had listed five topic areas. Next, I asked him to circle the ones that he was dearly interested in. Now, he circled three areas. We then looked at how each of these three topics related to what he had already written. We looked at the stated aim in his most recent introduction and then quickly sketched out the structure for each of the three topic areas. By doing this, Kevin could see which topic could be reasonably sustained in the time allotted for his Masters degree, and that he would not be able to tackle all five topics or even just the three he was interested in doing. He had to focus and discipline his thinking, and understand the constraints of the type of thesis he was trying to complete.

In a research project for a higher degree it is entirely normal to revise an aim, narrow or expand the scope of the study or discover that you may need fewer chapters than you initially envisaged. Your thinking will become more sophisticated as you gain confidence and authority through experience. For this reason we suggest that you look over your introductory chapter on a regular basis. Put it up on the screen, change a word here or there, check and refine the statement of the aim, add or delete limitations to the scope of the study and think about the overall structure. By doing this, you are likely to keep track of how you yourself are changing your thinking along the way, as opposed to being surprised that you have 'moved on' from a somewhat naive perspective. When your examiners read your thesis in a single sitting they will be impressed that the study has remained focused and has not drifted from start to conclusion. (Chapter 5 describes the sad outcome of a severe case of drift.)

Without focus, it is likely that you will never reach a critical appraisal of the literature. Your treatment of the background material will appear haphazard as it swerves from issue to issue in an attempt to cover a lot of ground. Examiners will be looking more for depth than for coverage.

Writing an individual chapter

How do you turn the literature reviews or descriptions of research procedures that you wrote in your first year into thesis chapters? You wrote them as stand-alone pieces, and when you wrote them you were not really on top of your subject.

Just as the thesis itself must be properly structured to ensure that the reader always knows exactly what is going on, so must individual chapters. Why is this particular chapter there? What is its function in the thesis? You must make this absolutely clear. The best way to ensure this is to write a formal introduction to every chapter. Follow this with the business of the chapter itself, then a formal conclusion. Many advisers consider this to be a rather stilted, over-formal approach, and skilful writers can certainly get away with no formal introductions and conclusions. This doesn't mean that they can do away with introductions and conclusions to chapters; rather that they do it less formally and obviously. Most of us don't have such writing skills, however, and we recommend that you write formal introductions and conclusions to all chapters.

What do we mean by a formal introduction? A simple rule worth following is that it should be made up of just three paragraphs, each with a specific function as shown in Box 4.

Paragraph 1: create a link back to earlier parts of the thesis, especially the previous chapter, to make it obvious why we need the chapter, where it contributes to the logic flow of the whole thesis.

Paragraph 2: crystallize this by stating the aim of the chapter, what *function* it is to perform in the thesis.

Paragraph 3: outline how you intend to achieve this aim. This third paragraph often has the 'table of contents' format that so many writers think constitutes an introduction. But it is only one part of the introduction, and without the other two parts the reader struggles for a sense of direction. (Incidentally, writers sometimes literally give it as a table of contents. This is far from helpful. The reader needs to know not only what you will be dealing with in the chapter, but also the logical connection between the various sections.)

Box 4: The three-paragraph rule for chapter introductions

Box 5 gives examples of how this rule might work out in practice.

INTRODUCTION FROM A TYPICAL BACKGROUND CHAPTER

'Chapter 3 A Different Approach: Privatisation', from the thesis An Approach to Improved Housing Delivery in Large Cities of Less Developed Countries by Alpana Sivam

One of the more important observations of Chapter 2 was that privatisation is spreading worldwide, both in developed and developing countries, as an alleged response to the problem of delivery of housing (including infrastructure) in large cities. Therefore it is likely to be prominent in any proposal for improving housing delivery in developing countries. For this reason it is important to understand what privatisation is, and why and how it is being applied to urban housing.

Section 3.1 defines privatisation. It then discusses the reason why governments are turning to it, and examines how it is being used and what effects it has had. Section 3.2 reviews its application to the housing sector. Section 3.3 examines the implications of these applications for housing delivery in developing countries.

INTRODUCTION FROM A CHAPTER DESCRIBING PART OF A CANDIDATE'S OWN WORK

'Chapter Four Government Intervention and Recycling', from the thesis Recycling Policy in Australia by Gina Hanson

It was suggested in Chapter three that government intervention aimed at encouraging manufacturers to use more reprocessed material when manufacturing product 'B' may be required to increase the quantity of material flowing through the recycling system [in Chapter three she had distinguished product A, which the consumer knows contains recycled material, from product B where the consumer does not know this]. Governments have already significantly intervened in recycling markets, for example by imposing

---

29

voluntary targets and waste pricing. However, as government intervention involves interference with normal market processes it should be undertaken with caution and with understanding of resultant economic outcomes.

This chapter examines different types of government intervention that have been used to increase recycling levels in order to determine which types of intervention are likely to work, and which types might be justifiable. To assist in this, some relevant microeconomic theory relating to market failure will first be reviewed. This theory will then be used to examine existing and proposed policies.

Box 5: Sample introductions to individual chapters

Note that in both introductions the three paragraphs we recommend have been compacted into two, although in each case the three elements are present.

You may be tempted to write far more than the three introductory paragraphs in your introductions, especially in background chapters. For example, the first draft of an introduction to a chapter reviewing approaches to the problem of housing in developing countries might include several pages describing the problem, as a prelude to reviews in later sections of the solutions proposed by various schools of thought. The readers will need this review, but if you give it to them before they learn why the chapter is in the thesis and what it is attempting to do you will confuse them. Make it the first section *after* your introduction.

After the introduction comes the main body of the chapter. Its precise contents and structure will depend on the type of chapter you are writing and the type of research you are reporting. Nevertheless, it is important that the chapter flows logically from its purpose, as stated in its introduction, to its conclusions. This typically involves three or four major sections. If you have more than six sections in a chapter, including the introduction and conclusion, you may be fairly sure that you haven't got the structure right.

Every chapter in a thesis should have a conclusion. The reader needs to share with the writer a sense of what has been achieved, what is established now that wasn't established at the beginning of the chapter. And the conclusion should, of course, respond to the stated aim or purpose of the chapter. There may be some exceptions, for example descriptive chapters outlining information on the characteristics of a study area. But chapters that should definitely have strong conclusions are reviews of theory, reviews of available research methods, reports of results, and the discussion (the conclusions here may constitute the conclusions to the whole thesis).

Students often have difficulty with conclusions. They tend to write summaries of what was in the chapter. A summary states *what* you found out, whereas a conclusion states the *significance* or *implications* of what you found out. (But don't get ahead of yourself. We have often found students reaching conclusions in background chapters that were informed by insights from their own work. Save this for your discussion chapter.) A conclusion has to respond to the statement of purpose of the chapter, whereas a summary is just a potted version of what is in the chapter. Box 6 shows the conclusion to Chapter four of Gina Hanson's thesis, the introduction of which was given in Box 5.

CONCLUSION TO A CHAPTER DESCRIBING PART OF A CANDIDATE'S OWN WORK

'Chapter Four Government Intervention and Recycling', from the thesis Recycling Policy in Australia by Gina Hanson

The economic theory considered here can in principle demonstrate that it is possible to determine a level of recycling which is most efficient for product B [the consumer is *not* aware that type B products contain recycled material]. There are also different types of government intervention which can assist in achieving this level when the market fails

---

to do so. However, a review of government intervention practices indicates that governments are presently implementing intervention policies to achieve levels of recycling that may not be economically or commercially optimal. The application of intervention policy to various recycling cases indicates that governments have not recognised the important difference between type A and type B products [the consumer *is* aware that type A products contain recycled material], and the different types of policy required to increase the recycling levels for these two types of product.

Economists such as Pearce and Tietenberg appear to have failed to recognise that their economic models and theories apply only to the situation of manufacturing products from substitutable reprocessed [type B] material. Confusion has resulted when these findings have been applied to community collection programs and the manufacture of products from unsubstitutable reprocessed [type A] materials.

Therefore, it would seem that Australian governments have so far not pursued the achievement of a socially optimal level of recycling as defined in microeconomic theory. Since government policy is not driven by financial or economic considerations, evidently it must be driven by other forces.

Box 6: Sample conclusions to a thesis chapter

You will notice that in the first paragraph Gina gives a very strong summary of the main findings of her analysis of government intervention. However, in the second and third paragraphs she goes far beyond reporting what she found out, and is quite clear about the implications of these findings. The conclusion in the third paragraph provides a strong lead into her next chapter, in which she attempts to find out what the 'other forces' she mentions might be. You might like to check to see whether her conclusions do respond to the aim she stated in her introduction, as given in Box 5.

SUMMARY

Your thesis should have the following structure:

1 An introductory chapter

- Tell the reader the problem you are tackling in this project.
- State clearly how you aim to deal with this problem.
- Limit the scope of your study.
- Sketch out how the thesis is structured to achieve this aim.

2 Background chapters

- Include in these chapters all the material required to lead up to your own work.
- Be critical, but do not conduct an indepth analysis. Keep this for section 4 below.

3 An account of your own work

- Begin with a formal statement of your hypotheses or research questions.
- Follow this with an account of the methods you chose to test your hypotheses or answer your questions, and why you chose them.
- Then report the results of applying these methods.

4 Synthesis

- You are now ready to pull the whole thesis together.
- Discuss the implications of your results.
- Modify existing theory (as reported in section 2) or develop new theory.
- Draw strong conclusions backed up by your discussion.
- Check that they respond to the aim stated in section 1.

Starting your thesis

- Write early, and write often. Keep your research in parallel with your writing so they both develop critically.
- Don't put off starting the writing process too long. If you do delay writing until after you have done your own

work, make sure that you are writing to the strong structure advocated above.

- Start with confidence: Write your introductory chapter first, then put it aside while you work on other parts of your study. Come back from time to time to revise your aim and scope so that they align with the changes you are making as you go along.

Structuring individual chapters

- Start with an introduction that tells the reader why this chapter is included in the thesis, what you intend to achieve in it, and how you intend to do this.
- Develop the chapter in an appropriate and logical way to achieve the aim stated in the introduction.
- Write a formal conclusions section. Make sure that it is not a summary of the contents of the chapter, but rather a strong statement of the implications of the findings.
- Check that you have argued for the conclusions in the body of the chapter.
- Check that these conclusions respond to the aim stated in the introduction to the chapter.

4 Making your word processor work for you

When researchers first began to use word processors, they used them rather like typewriters: they still wrote a manuscript by hand, and handed it to the typist for typing. But now they had the luxury of treating the typescript as a draft that could easily be changed—by marking it up and handing it back to the typist for revision.

All this has changed. Most academics now do all their own word processing. Most undergraduate students produce their assignments on word processors. All of our research students have prepared their theses using word processors for some years now. Many professional consultants and officers in government departments produce all but the final versions of their reports on word processors at their own desks. This has profoundly affected the way research can be carried out and reported.

We are assuming in this chapter that you have basic knowledge of how to operate word-processing applications. To produce a good thesis, however, you will need far more than this so that you can take advantage of features built into your word processor that will make your work more effective and more efficient. In this chapter we will suggest how to get the best out of your word processor; to make it work for you.*

Presentation

Consider what software engineers thought about as they created word-processing programs. They didn't just sit down at their desks and say, 'Wouldn't it be nice to write this feature or that capability into our program'. Instead, they had many sessions with experienced writers, typists, typesetters, book editors and so on, and listed all the features that might be desirable. They than estimated the computer memory that might be required, and put the features in some order of priority. This led them to reject some features that were desirable but not feasible within the constraints of available computer power, and they finally produced a program that embodied the best combination of desirable features at that time. Experience by users revealed the limitations of the program and, as computer power increased, the programmers produced new versions that overcame the problems, and built in new features. We have now reached the stage where programs are so sophisticated that it is almost beyond the power of single individuals to make use of all the features. We have laboured this point to indicate that you should approach the learning of the capabilities of programs by saying, 'This is what I want to do; I know the programmers will have provided me with the capability. All I have to do is find it.'

Nowhere is this more apparent than in the question of presentation. The program can't do your creative thinking for

---

* Descriptions of features of word-processing programs in this chapter refer to Microsoft®Word 2000 for Windows®. Other advanced programs will have similar features, but they may be described and accessed somewhat differently.

you (not yet, anyway!), but it is very good at helping you to get things down in a good and clear format. Programs now check your spelling for you, and make suggestions about your grammar. They can also do footnotes for you, and help you with your list of references and your table of contents.

Before thinking about the technology, think about the style and format you are going to adopt. In theory, you have great latitude in your choices, so long as you are consistent in what you do. In practice, however, we suggest that you go to the top journals in your field to see how they format published work. Next, talk with your supervisor about the most widely used style manual in your field. (Many of the applied sciences, for example, tend to use the American Psychological Association (APA) *Publication Manual*.) Once you determine what style your readership is likely to be familiar with, get a copy of the manual and learn its conventions.

Once you have established a pattern, stick to it, and the reader will get the same message every time. For example, main section headings, wherever they appear in your document, should always be in the same typeface, of the same size and the same character (bold, italic or whatever). They should always be preceded by the same space separation from preceding text, and always be followed by the same space separation. If the style you choose is clearly different from that for other headings, the reader will quickly understand 'We are starting a new main section' or, 'This is a sub-section within the section'. This is especially true if you use a style that is familiar to most readers in the field.

Creating and using a thesis template

A thesis consists of several different parts that need to be tied together with a set of conventions. Without a standard format across the entire document, the work will appear random and unprofessional. For example, you should put all chapter headings on a new page, using the same style, i.e. the same font and paragraphing.* You should give all major section headings a style that is different from that of the chapter headings (one that is less prominent). Captions to figures should all have the same style, but different again from section headings. All new paragraphs should have the same space before them, and should begin with the same indent (except for the first paragraph after a heading, which may have no indent at all), and so on. All this will help your readers to navigate their way through your thesis.

Before you start typing anything for your report or thesis, you should think about its format, and devise styles and formatting rules that are appropriate for your field of study. Above all, make up your mind that, right from the outset, you will not use just any old style, with a view to tightening things up later when you are more confident about what you are doing. Begin as you mean to continue.

Fortunately, most current word-processing programs have a feature built into them that will help you to do this, while keeping the flexibility to change your styles later if you wish. It is called a *template*. This is how to make a template in Word for Windows 2000.† First, open up a blank document and type out the words 'Heading 1', press the *Enter* (Return) key, and then 'Heading 2', press *Enter*, 'Heading 3' and so on. Every time you press the *Enter* key you start a new paragraph, as signified by the ¶ symbol (it's a good idea to always keep these markers switched on). Try to think of all the different ways that you might want to format different parts of your text, such as chapter headings, section

---

* Font refers to the typeface, e.g. Ariel or Times; its size, e.g. 12 point or 24 point; and its character, e.g. regular, bold or italic. Paragraphing refers to the spaces before and after the paragraph; the indent (if any); the alignment, e.g. aligned to the left or right or centred, or justified (each line going to both margins).

† If you are using another program, you will need to find your way around it so that you can do the things we talk about in the following pages. The same point applies in later chapters that refer to Word 2000.

headings, sub-section headings, normal text, block quotations, captions to figures, dot-point lists and numbered lists, and type in words for all of these, each in its separate paragraph. Now you have to give each of these different forms of text its own style. To do this, use the mouse to set the locator on one of the words you have typed. Go to the *Format* menu and select *Style*. The Style Box that appears will incorporate a list of default styles built into your program. Click on the one you want. For example if your locator is on the word 'Heading 1' click on the style *Heading 1*. If you now click on *Apply* you will impose the program's default style on the paragraph 'Heading 1'. If you don't like the default style, modify it by following the instructions in the Style Box. For example, if you wished to use the style used for chapter headings in the APA *Publication Manual* to format *Heading 1,* set it so that it is centred and can contain both upper and lower case letters. Repeat this process for all the other words you have typed in, 'Heading 2', 'Heading 3', 'Normal' etc. If the style you want is not on the list of default styles (for example you might want a *Tabulation* style for making entries in tables in slightly smaller type than usual), create a new style as indicated in the Style Box.

When you have completed all of the styles you want for the moment (you can add more later), save the blank document as a template, which you might call 'Thesis Styles' or 'Thesis Template'. This template is a standard document with a standard set of styles built into it. Now that you have established the template, use it each time you begin a new chapter. To do this, open the 'Thesis Styles' template and save as 'Chapter 1' or 'Chapter 2' or whatever you are working on.* Then start typing. When you want to write the chapter title click on the style *Heading 1* in the style selector box in the Format toolbar. Type your chapter title

---

* In Word for Windows 2000 you open a blank document containing the template styles by double clicking the template. If you select the template and click on *Open* you will open the template itself, and can then alter the styles in the template.

and press *Enter*. Every time you want to type a section heading, click on the style *Heading 2* in the style selector box, and the paragraph you are typing will automatically adopt the *Heading 2* style. When you press the *Enter* (Return) key to start a new paragraph the style of the next paragraph will also be chosen, usually as *Normal,* but you can change this by using the Style Box, which is viewed by selecting *Style* from the *Format* menu.

Any paragraph can be reformatted with any style by clicking somewhere on the paragraph, then clicking on the desired style on the style selector box on the Format toolbar. In this way you can ensure that all text paragraphs in every chapter will always have the same indenting and the same space between them; all section headings will be in exactly the same style, and so on.

We have gone into this in some detail, because if you have never used a template before the idea will be quite foreign to you. Do not skip this: it is the single most important feature of your word processor, and you must learn how to use it properly. Spend an hour or two, with a document open in front of you, playing with the Style Box from the *Style* command in the *Format* menu and the style selector box in the Format toolbar until you get it right. We describe below a few of the things you can do if you use a template with your own selected styles.

First, suppose you decide, when you print out a sample page or so, that the section headings are not really the way you want them. Since you have given all section headings the same style, say *Heading 2,* all you have to do is re-specify this style into the desired format, using the Style Box. Every paragraph you have labelled *Heading 2* will automatically be changed to the new *Heading 2* style.

Next, you can generate a Table of Contents for the document you have open (if you haven't labelled your headings with heading styles this won't work). Just select the *Index and Tables* command from the *Insert* menu. Then select *Table of Contents* and click on the number of levels of heading that you want and click on *OK.* A Table of Contents will magically appear where your locator bar was placed (make sure that it was not in the middle of your document before you start!). We shall say more about tables of contents later in this chapter.

Finally, the use of styles allows you to use the powerful *Outline* command (if you haven't labelled your headings with heading styles this also won't work). If you always stay with the program's default view (usually Print Layout view), you will never be able to see the entire structure of your work at a single glance. Three very powerful features are built into the Outline view:

- Simple mouse or keyboard instructions permit you to suppress as much of the hierarchy of headings as you wish. For example, you could hide all the ordinary text and leave only the headings. Or you could hide, in addition, all the sub-section headings, leaving only the section headings and the chapter headings. Or you could hide all but the chapter headings. This feature enables you to see very clearly the structure of the document you are working on, and to identify problems such as repetitions and gaps in logic.

- You can insert additional headings in response to these problems, or move sections or even chapters around to improve the logic flow. You can also promote or demote a heading to a different level in the hierarchy. You can do this after you have hidden any ordinary text to help you to see quite clearly what you are doing. But whenever you move a heading from one place to another, or promote or demote it, it takes with it all its subsidiary material that you have temporarily hidden. When you have finished all of this rearranging, you can switch back to Print Layout view, and you will see that it has all been rearranged. No doubt you will then have to do some editorial work to tidy up the logic. When you have attempted this, you may find that what seemed like a good idea won't really work. Just switch back to Outline view and reverse the whole process, or try something else.

- Your Outline view can give you a draft Table of Contents. You can try just chapter and section headings, or you can call up the sub-section headings also, and see whether you improve the Table of Contents or make it worse.

Key features of your word-processing program

Once you have mastered styles and templates, it is time to move on to some other key features that are found in most modern word processing programs. But be warned: some of them will not work unless you have used styles properly, so make sure that you have mastered styles and devised a template.

Spell-checks and grammar-checks

Most word-processing programs include a facility for checking spelling. It checks every word you have typed against a dictionary built into the program. If it can't find the word (either because the word is not in the program's dictionary or because you have spelt it wrongly—sometimes because you have inadvertently omitted the space between two words), it will give you a warning, usually by underlining in red. You can respond either by ignoring the warning, or by accepting the invitation to change the word to a preferred spelling. Do not ignore it! Very few people are infallible spellers or proof-readers. It is as well to have oddities questioned.

However, although the spell-check is very good at picking up typographical errors, it can't make decisions for you. Typical problems are proper names (people's names or place names), and words for which there are alternative spellings. In the case of proper names, the temptation is to tell the program to ignore its questionings, and go instead to the next area of doubt. This is a mistake. You should check any proper name the first time the spell-check comes to it and, when you are satisfied that you have got it right, add it to the dictionary installed in the program. The second problem is words for which alternative spellings are permissible (*-or* or *-our,* and *-ize* or *-ise* are the most common). The most important constraint here is that you must be consistent. Before you start, determine your preferred spellings for these words, and keep to them.

On a related note, don't rely on the spell-check to proof-read for you; although it will pick up misspelt words, it won't distinguish between, for example, *there* and *their,* or *affect* and *effect.* Similarly, it won't tell you if you have left a word out.

A grammar-check, which is contained in the most recent programs, may also help. Grammar-checks operate a bit like spell-checks. They look at every sentence, and make checks such as: does it contain a verb; is it too long and complicated; does the subject agree with the verb (plural subjects must not have singular verbs); is the verb in the passive voice (permissible, but should be used sparingly); are stock phrases being used (examples: 'over and above', 'in order to', 'part and parcel'), and so on. If you are breaking any of the grammar check's rules it will give you a warning, usually by underlining, but this time in green. You may think that your English is better than the grammar check's English, and decide to ignore its warnings. Our experience is that the checks in the latest programs are so good that it is usually wise to try to get rid of those wavy green lines by breaking the sentence up or rearranging it.

References

At present the *name and year* (or *Harvard*) system is the most popular reference system for theses. Your word-processing program will help you to use this system, in conjunction with a reference database built up by either yourself or your organization using a program such as Endnote. In this program you build up a catalogue of references much like the old card-index system used by a previous generation of researchers. Each entry consists of the usual listing of author, title of article and journal, or of book or chapter of book, year of publication, and publisher and place, together with an abstract and keywords. This reference database can be used quite independently of your thesis as a personal literature recording and accessing device (using author's name or keywords or title of book or journal to search for material). However, it also has the great advantage that you can interface it with your thesis to insert references in the text and automatically draw up the list of references you have inserted at the end.

The most important alternative referencing system is the *numbered note* system, which is used in many books. Word-processing programs usually have this referencing system built into them. You can stop at any point and (if you are using Word 2000) insert a note by using the *Insert Footnote* command (most word-processing programs call them footnotes rather than notes, because the default setting does collect them at the foot of each page). You can give notes a number or symbol yourself, or you can ask the program to automatically number them, which is preferable. The number (or symbol) will appear as a superscript in the text, and also as a duplicate on a separate part of the screen. You are invited to type in the text of your note against this duplicate number or symbol. The numbered note system is more versatile than the Harvard system, as it can be used not only for references but also for comments or explanations that you don't wish to put in the text because they break the logic flow. Where you are using it for references you can once again use Endnote to help you.

If later you wish to add another note higher up on the same page, all you have to do is insert a new note marker in the text. The notes will automatically renumber themselves, and you simply type in the text for the new note on the separate part of the screen. Conversely, if you delete an existing reference number from the main text, the note text that went with it will also be automatically deleted, and the other notes will be renumbered automatically. This renumbering facility is now making the numbered note system more popular for theses— one of the advantages of the Harvard system was that you could delete or add references without the need for renumbering.

But check—some university departments still insist on the Harvard system. And, as we remarked earlier, you may wish to write your thesis in the style that publications in your area use, and that will include using their reference system.

Notes are usually collected at the end of each page as footnotes. When the page is printed out you will see the superscript number in the main text and the footnote text at the bottom of the page, separated from the main text by a dividing line. If you have more than one reference number on the page, the footnotes will all be collected automatically on that page. However, if you wish, you may instead collect the notes at the end of a section (for example, at the end of each chapter) or in a consolidated listing at the end of your thesis.

Wherever you put them, the notes have to be backed up by a consolidated alphabetical listing of all the references in them. A typical PhD thesis will have two hundred or more references. Keeping track of these is a daunting task. For this reason alone it is worth learning how to use Endnote. While it is putting the reference in the text it is also preparing a list of references to put at the end of the document. If you do not wish to use Endnote, copy all your numbered notes containing a reference in them on to a separate section at the end of your document labelled 'References'. It is then a relatively simple matter to later convert all the references in this document to a listing with authors' names first and then, using the *Sort* command (usually in the *Table* menu), to generate a list of references in alphabetical order. When you have finished your thesis you can consolidate all the chapters into one document or keep them separate if you wish (see later in this chapter). If you keep them separate, you will have to paste all the chapter lists of references into a single document labelled 'References'.

Whichever system of referencing you use, the word processor offers the advantage that it will help you to maintain the match between the references cited in the text and the references appearing in your consolidated alphabetical list of references. It will help to prevent you from inadvertently omitting references from your list that have been referred to in the text, and will also help to prevent you from retaining references in the list that are no longer referred to in the text. It will also automatically sort them into alphabetical order.

Tables

Most word-processing applications have routines for constructing tables. As it takes some time to learn how to use these routines properly, you might be tempted to abandon the attempt to use them, and to construct the tables using tabs. However, if you are going to construct an appreciable number of tables, it is worth spending time to master the table routines. Be sure you follow the guidelines that are found in your style manual. If you have done the tables properly, you will be able to change the typeface or size without risking a disaster, as you would with tabs. (Rarely does one see a report without at least one entry having been displaced to the wrong column; this just won't happen if you use a table routine.)

You should construct your captions to tables by using (in Word 2000) the *Insert Caption* command. Not only will this ensure that all captions are in the same style, but your program will have a facility built into it for automatically numbering the tables. If you delete a table later, or insert an extra one, the facility will automatically renumber the captions (you should also be able to make it renumber references to them in the text, but this is a bit more tricky to use, so take care). You may wish to have all tables for a particular chapter identified as such (for example, if you are going to keep the chapters separate at the end). In this case, tables in Chapter 3, for example, would be labelled Table 3.1, Table 3.2 etc. *Insert Caption* will readily manage this for you.

Figures

You will sometimes find theses in your library with all the figures collected together at the end of each chapter, each on a separate page. This was another product of the typewriter age; you won't find them like that in a book. The word processor enables you to enter them in much the same way as in a book: as close as you can get them to the place where they are first mentioned in the written text, and not on a separate page from the text. There are four ways of doing this:

- If your word-processing package has a reasonably sophisticated graphical routine built into it, you might consider using it to draw some or all of your figures. This method has the advantage that you can edit the figures at a later date in the light of rewriting or alteration of the text. However, you will have to accept the limitations of the graphics routine, which might be quite considerable.

- If you are using charts generated by a spreadsheet program such as Microsoft®Excel you can import these electronically into your text. If you want to plot your own data it is worth entering them into a spreadsheet and getting the program to plot them for you. Such programs will display your data in a variety of useful formats.

- You can draw all your figures using a separate specialist graphics package, and import them electronically into your text. You will not be able to edit them while they are in your word-processed text—but you can delete them, go back to the original version in the graphics package, edit that, then re-import it.

- You can draw all your figures by hand on separate sheets of paper, using a consistent graphical style. Then scan the figures electronically and import these electronically into your text. Again, you cannot edit these and, if you wish to change them, you will have to redraw them. The method of scanning has the advantage that you can copy material from various sources as well as drawing your own. But remember to acknowledge the source of any such drawings—copying without proper acknowledgement is called plagiarism, which is a form of stealing.

Whichever method you use, you should go to some trouble to ensure consistency of style within the figures, especially if there is written material actually on the figures themselves, such as labels on the axes of graphs. You should produce the captions of all your figures, together with any explanatory material and references to sources, in a consistent style, using your word-processing package. Don't attempt to do these graphically. As for tables, use the (Word 2000) *Insert Caption* command to construct your captions. However, whereas it is customary to put the caption to a table above the table, it is customary to put the caption to a figure below it.

Table of Contents

A *Table of Contents* is a list of what is contained in the thesis. It usually includes the titles of each chapter, with a *very* brief listing under each title of what is in the chapter. It functions as a map of the thesis—what is in it, how its various parts relate to each other, and how to find your way around it. It is placed at the front of the thesis, and you may expect it to be read first. The table of contents should not be confused with an *Index*, which is a listing of important words and ideas appearing in the work, given in alphabetical order. Its function is to help anyone to check whether a subject they are interested in is dealt with in the work and, if it is, to find it. An index is located at the end of the work, and will not be read before the work itself; in fact, it is unlikely to be read systematically at all. The most recent word-processing programs have routines for generating both tables of contents and indexes. We shall discuss only tables of contents here, as it is most unusual to have an index in a thesis (this is because a thesis is not being read as a textbook, the function of which is to inform the reader about something, but rather as an examination paper).

As we noted earlier, if you give your chapter titles the style *Heading 1,* your section headings the style *Heading 2,* your subsection headings the style *Heading 3,* and so on, you can use the command *Insert Index and Tables* in your program to print out a table of contents from these headings. This can be done at any level of detail you wish—for example, you might include only chapter headings and section headings, or you might also include sub-section headings. This facility automatically lists the page number on which each heading occurs. If you make any changes after generating your table of contents the page numbering may be upset, so you should remember to run the table-of-contents routine again, right at the end.

If you have looked over a number of theses, you will have noted that each of them contains a list of tables and figures. Your word-processing application can make this list automatically through the use (in Word 2000) of the *List of Figures* facility found in the *Insert Index and Tables* command. This will only work if you have used the *Insert Captions* command to produce the captions.

Tracking changes

You will find the *Track Changes* command in the *Tools* menu in Word 2000. It allows you to alter a document, see what you have done, and later decide whether to 'accept' or 'reject' your decisions. It can be used collaboratively for documents with a number of multiple authors (see Chapter 12). We recommend that you take note of it and learn to use it, as it may come in handy during particular points in your thesis. We suggest, however, that you do not overuse the feature: often, students worry too much about every word they have typed to the detriment of their creative processes. Before you implement the feature, make a distinction between when you are writing creatively and when you are hard at work on crucial revisions.

Putting it all together

If you keep the chapters as separate documents, to turn them into a single thesis you will have to renumber the starting page of every chapter manually, and make your table of contents by making individual tables for each chapter and pasting them into a consolidated list. You will have to begin a new list of figures and tables for each chapter, and again copy the individual components of these from each chapter and paste them into a consolidated list. All of this is tedious, and provides many opportunities for making errors.

It is preferable to bring all of the chapters together so that page numbering will be continuous, and so that (in Word 2000) the *Table of Contents, List of Figures* and *List of Tables* commands will all operate on the whole thesis. There are two ways of doing this. The most obvious way is to copy and paste each chapter into a 'complete thesis' document prepared from your thesis template. A preferable method is to use the 'Master Document' facility, which you will find in the more recent programs. In both cases, if you have not prepared each chapter from the thesis template you will get into a tangle, which you will now have to sort out.

If you decide to use the master document facility, first orientate yourself by looking over the section on 'master document' in the online *Help* facility. Then create a Master Document using the same template that you have used for each of the chapters. Now, add your various chapters to this document one at a time (in Word 2000) using the *Insert Subdocument* command in *Outline* view. The Master Document will begin to look like one long *Outline* view, with each chapter clearly delineated by a break. Note that it is now very easy to create a table of contents, a list of tables and a list of figures, because all of the pages have been automatically numbered. The entire document should also have a consistent format. To save, use the *Save As* feature under the *File* menu to name your newly created Master Document.

Although the master documents facility helps manage long files, it is easy to get confused by it. For example, it only works if all of the chapters are available on the same computer. This occurs because the Master Document is really only an empty shell—it doesn't save your chapters inside itself, it only draws upon them. If all else fails, use the information about master documents in the *Help* menu or consult a knowledgeable colleague.

Document management

University lecturers have become accustomed over the years to all the standard excuses that students have invented for not submitting assignments on time. The word processor has spawned a completely new set, mostly to do with poor disk or document management. The great slave can become an obstinate enemy! If you follow a few simple rules you will avoid the most common problems.

Saving and duplicates

When you type material you are storing large amounts of information in the electronic circuitry of your computer (not in its hard disk, which we shall return to shortly). The storages consist of millions of electronic switches, each of which is in the *on* or the *off* position. As you operate the keyboard you are instructing certain switches to be turned on, and it is the pattern of *ons* and *offs* that the word-processing program interprets as letters and numbers arranged on the page. If the power supply to the computer is turned off, for example through a power failure, or because the program 'freezes' and the only way to get it going again is to switch off the computer and start again, all these switches will be turned off, and the material you have typed will be lost. To store this information permanently, you have to transfer a copy of the pattern of *ons* and *offs* to a magnetized disk. This process is called *saving* to the disk. There are three different types of disk. Your computer has a *hard disk* built into it, with a very large capacity for storing material, usually called *memory*. After some time you will find yourself, consciously or unconsciously, using the hard disk as an electronic filing cabinet. It may also be equipped with a slot for inserting a portable *floppy disk,* which has far less memory, but which has the advantage that it can be removed from the computer and kept separate from it. Many computers can also make use of a *Zip disk*®,* which also can be separated from the computer, but has far more memory than a floppy disk. You may also have a fourth means of saving your work. If your computer is connected to a server—a remote computer that stores files—you may be able to save your work there.

Separable disks and servers can be used to transfer information from one computer to another. They can also be used to keep a duplicate of any document (a 'backup'), against the day when your hard disk fails in some way (uncommon, but does happen), or more commonly when you accidentally delete a document.

As the first problem, loss of power while you are working, is not uncommon, it is advisable to save the document you are working on frequently. Most programs automatically save to the hard disk every few minutes. You can set the time yourself to allow the best compromise between time lost by saving too often, and information lost if you happened to lose power. Most people go for five minutes. However, you should realize that when you save your document on to the disk you automatically delete the earlier version of it on the disk by overwriting it with the new version. For example, if you are playing around with extensive editing of a document called 'Ch 8 Discussion' and have saved once or twice, then decide you don't like the new version after all, you will have lost the original ('Somehow I lost half the stuff on my disk'). Therefore, if you have any doubts as to whether you might want to keep the earlier version, make a copy of it before you begin editing by using the 'Save As' command under the 'File' menu in Word 2000 and name it 'Ch 8 DiscussionA' before you continue writing. This is probably

---

* Zip is a registered trademark of Iomega Corporation.

quite routine for you by now, but it becomes an important problem again when you start working on a joint paper (see Chapter 12). The only way to deal with the second problem, the loss of a document on the hard disk, or even the loss of the whole hard disk itself, is to always back up your documents on a floppy disk, a Zip disk or remote server before you close your computer down after a work session. Store these duplicates separately from your computer—if a thief should steal your computer (not uncommon with laptops) you could lose your whole thesis.

Using more than one computer

You probably have access to a computer at the university as well as your own computer at home. You might do some work on a document on your home computer, then some more work on the same document on the computer at the university. To do this, you will have made a copy of the document on a floppy disk, a Zip disk or remote server for access from home to the university. Most computer experts say that it is sound practice to build up your master document on your hard disk rather than on a floppy disk, because a hard disk is less likely to break down than a portable disk. The floppy or Zip then contains a duplicate of the document made before you closed the home computer down. You then transfer this copy to the hard disk of the computer at the university to do further work. But if you do this you will end up with two separate masters on two separate hard disks, and the distinct possibility of overwriting a master document with the copy on the portable disk. There are quite a few ways of dealing with this problem, but you must think them through and devise strict rules for dealing with it.

My solution is to make the floppy disk or the Zip disk the master disk, and risk the possibility that it might break down one day ('My disk blew up'). As you will see in a moment, even if this were to happen, it would not be a big disaster. It works like this. You are about to start your thesis on your home computer, and decide to start with a draft of 'Chapter 3: Theory'. Open your template 'Thesis Template' and save as 'Ch 3 Theory'. Take a floppy or Zip disk, insert it in your home computer, format it, and call it 'Thesis 1'. This is your master disk. Copy 'Ch 3 Theory' on to it from your hard disk and put it aside. Now type as much of Chapter 3 in the document 'Ch 3 Theory' on your home computer as you wish. Save, close the document, and copy this version of it from your hard disk on to your master floppy or Zip disk. This will over-ride the version you already had on the floppy disk. You now have the latest version of your document 'Ch 3 Theory' on your master disk (the floppy or Zip disk). This is the master document. You also have a copy of it on your home hard disk so that if the floppy or Zip 'blows up' you still have a copy of the latest version of the master document at home.

You now take the master floppy or Zip disk, 'Thesis 1', to the university, insert it in your university computer and copy the latest version of your master document 'Ch 3 Theory' on to it. Do some more work on this document on your hard disk and, when you have finished for the day save, close the document and copy the latest version of 'Ch 3 Theory' on to your master floppy or Zip disk. You now have two copies of your latest version of 'Ch 3 Theory', one on the university hard disk, and one on your master disk, the floppy or Zip. You take the floppy or Zip home, insert it in the home computer, copy 'Ch 3 Theory' on to the home hard disk to overwrite the previous version, and do further work on it. Save, close down, and copy this latest version of your 'Ch 3 Theory' back on to the master floppy or Zip disk. And so on.

If you do not have sole control of the work computer, and therefore cannot safely leave a copy of your latest version of 'Ch 3 Theory' on it, you could take a copy on a duplicate floppy or Zip. I think it better not to do this, as one day you will get the duplicate and the master muddled (in my experience this is the most common cause of the puzzled statement, 'Somehow I lost a lot of stuff on my disk').

If your computer at the university does not accept a floppy or Zip disk, make sure that you learn to back up work through online networked resources. A number of departments, for example, provide students with access to a central server. At our university, this departmental server is then regularly backed up to larger computers. Beyond the university environment, you may wish to explore the possibility of using 'virtual hard drives' that are available through a number of sources over the Internet. We don't wish to make any specific recommendations, and cannot vouch for their security, but several of our students have reported using them without any problems. To begin your exploration, type in the phrase 'virtual hard drive' into an Internet search engine and go from there. Critically evaluate the services by looking for how much space is being offered (25MB is standard), whether the service is well known, and whether you will be required to pay. Be alert for the 'fine print', especially if you are asked to receive 'junk email' as part of your use of the service.

Interacting with your supervisor

Whenever you prepare a document for your supervisor, such as a review on a topic or a draft chapter, make sure that you label it in the header and/or the footer with the following: page number (yes, it is easy to forget); the name of the document (and give it a name that clearly identifies it—it is really annoying for a supervisor to receive a document merely labelled 'Draft Chapter 3', and not know whose Draft Chapter 3 it is); your name (your supervisor no doubt has more than one student); and the date (otherwise you and your supervisor will get tangled up with which version of Chapter 3 it is). This problem becomes really acute if you are sending your supervisor material by email attachment. If you are giving your supervisor a hard copy it is also a good idea to start with a Table of Contents of the document.

SUMMARY

Get to know your word processor

- Develop a template based on the most common style in your field.
- Use the template each time you begin a new chapter.
- Utilize 'Outline' view to see an overview of your structure.

Learn key features

- Learn how to do footnotes.
- If possible, enrol in a course on Endnote.
- Make sure you have mastered all aspects of your *Tables* facility.
- See how far the graphics package in your application can help you.
- Learn how to import graphic material from other applications or from scans of drawings or photographs
- Use the *Insert Captions* command (Word 2000) to help you number figures and tables.
- Use the *Insert Index and Tables* command (Word 2000) to draw up Tables of Contents, Lists of Tables and Lists of Figures.
- Learn *Track Changes* (Word 2000), but do not use it so much that it stifles your drafting process.

Document management

- If you are using more than one computer, develop a systematic method for determining what constitutes the 'master' copy of your document.
- Always label draft documents with the document name, your name, page numbers and the date. Start the document with a Table of Contents.
- Consider the use of networked computers for backing up your work.

5 The introductory chapter

I was chairman of the examination board for Graham's thesis. It was one of the most frustrating experiences I have ever had, and must have been far worse for Graham. His supervisor had suggested that he investigate a tricky applied engineering problem concerned with the flow of a particular plastic substance. As he was an excellent mathematician, he decided to look at the previous derivations of the equations governing such flows. He discovered that the standard solution given in the specialist books on the subject was a special case of a more general solution, and that generalizing this standard solution to all such flows could lead to errors. He ended up writing a brilliant thesis on applied mathematics, quite different from his original intention. But he had written his introductory chapter before the project took a different turn, and had neglected to rewrite it. The examiners sent the thesis back for rewriting. The introduction threw them so far off the track that they failed to realize what a brilliant piece of work he had done.

I hope this cautionary tale has impressed you. Graham had done one of the best pieces of research that I have a detailed knowledge of, but it was to no avail—he had messed up the introductory chapter.

The introduction is the shortest but the most important chapter in your thesis. It can make or break it. It has only one function: to introduce readers to the thesis. Make sure that it does this. First, tell them why the research is worth tackling—what the problem is, why it is important. End this statement of your research problem with a single sentence stating your overall research aim, which should grow out of your problem statement. You should be able to start the statement of your aim with the word 'thus' or 'therefore'. In many cases it will be necessary to elaborate on this aim by putting some limits or constraints on it. If you need to do this, start a new paragraph. You are not adding more aims; what you are doing is limiting the scope of your investigation. Then give a brief overview of how the thesis is laid out, and why it is laid out in this way. You should be able to start this section with the words, 'To achieve this aim, Chapter 2 does so and so . . . Then Chapter 3 does . . .', and so on.

What else should be in the introduction? Our advice is not to burden it with any other functions at all: no review of the literature, no statement of theory, no glossary of terms. If you want to include these in your thesis, put them somewhere else. Make the introduction an uncluttered and absolutely clear statement of what you are attempting. If it has only three pages and other chapters have twenty pages, don't worry. They have different functions.

Problem statement

The first page or so of your thesis describes why you thought it was worth spending three years of your life on your chosen topic. We have given this short opening section the title 'Problem statement', because your research is nearly always an attempt to find a solution to a problem that you have identified. You believe that the present way of doing things is inadequate in some way, or that existing theory does not explain the observable behaviour of a system satisfactorily. Sometimes to call it a problem may be too strong: for example, if you were a historian you might be looking for a new way to view a series of events or the place of a particular person in them. In this case you would choose a milder term such as 'Background to the study'. But don't omit this critical opening section. The examiner wants to know the driving force behind your research.

What should be in it? Certainly not a full review of the literature, although there might be some reference to it, because the unsatisfactory state of theory or practice might well be the problem—the justification for carrying out the work to be described. Box 7 shows my favourite problem statement. It is just two paragraphs long. It is in a masters thesis written by Geoff Thomas, under my supervision, entitled The Ignition of Brown Coal Particles.

Over half the energy used in the world today is obtained from coal, mostly through the combustion of pulverized coal. Despite a great accumulation of empirical information since the first trials in 1818 very little has been discovered about the detailed mechanism of the combustion of pulverized coal.

In Victoria, the indigenous brown coal is being used to provide much of the state's energy, mostly through the combustion of pulverized brown coal in power station boilers. Although the first such trials were carried out in the 1920s no study of the fundamentals of pulverized brown coal combustion has been reported. This represents a serious gap in the knowledge required for the efficient use of pulverized brown coal.

Box 7: A sample problem statement

You will note that there is no review of literature or theory here (he did review it later in his thesis), merely a simple justification that here was a very large problem that was worth putting some effort into.*

The problem statement is the context of the research, the reason it was worth tackling, the precursor to the research aim. You will have to elaborate on it later in the document, for example in the review of current theory, but not here.

Aim

Alastair McLauchlan had read about my view of the aim of a thesis in the first edition of this book, and emailed me for help.† He was examining discrimination against the *burakumin*, an underprivileged group in Japan whose ancestors were outcasts because they worked in the unclean leather and butchery industries. He couldn't work out what he was trying to do in the whole project, even though he had written the background chapters and had prepared a paper for an international journal based on one of them. Box 8 shows the research aim he had written.

> The aim of the research is to establish which groups of mainstream Japanese continue to harbour anti-burakumin attitudes, analyse what those attitudes are and why they have remained extant, and to suggest which political measures are needed to solve the problem.

Box 8: An example of a multiple aim

You will see that he actually had announced four aims in the same sentence:

---

* He turned out to be right. The work done by him and others who followed, using his techniques and ideas, did assist the State Electricity Commission of Victoria in designing brown coal burners by methods other than expensive, and sometimes dangerous, trial and error.

† We appreciate Alastair's generosity in agreeing to share his experiences with other readers.

- To establish which groups of mainstream Japanese continue to harbour anti-burakumin attitudes;
- To analyse what these attitudes are;
- To determine why they have remained extant; and
- To suggest what political measures are needed to solve the problem.

What was the real aim? Almost certainly it was the last one. The other three were steps in the research method. He knew that he would not be able to make any suggestions about how 'the problem' could be solved unless he knew where it lay, and why it had persisted from the 1870s to this day. His problem statement would need to outline the problem step by step: that the Japanese government had formally declared these people to be outcasts in the 1870s; that their outcast status had become entrenched by custom until after World War II and that, as a result, they were discriminated against in education, employment, social welfare and marriage; that the government in 1969 passed legislation to attempt to bring the social status of these people up to mainstream norms; but that, despite this, discrimination, although not as marked and no longer government policy, was still quite persistent. Thus the 'problem' was to find what an enlightened government might do next. Alastair needed to state that his aim was to solve this problem, not to tell the reader *how* he was going to solve it. The first three of his 'aims' should not appear until his research design chapter (see Chapter 7). And, having identified the problem, he needs to say what he means by 'solving' it: in this case 'to identify ways in which the Japanese government could improve the social status of the burakumin'.

Your stated aim should have three characteristics:

- It should follow as a logical consequence of the problem statement. You identify a problem; your aim is to solve it (but, as just noted, you have to be clear about what the problem is).
- It should be singular. You must identify only one aim. This is not easy to do. Students often show magnificent ingenuity in stringing all the aims they want to include into the same

sentence, as Alastair had. But four aims in the one sentence are still four aims. Nearly always some of the excess aims are in fact steps in the method that you have already unconsciously been working on to achieve that one true aim. If we were permitted to give only one piece of advice to students writing theses, it would be this: stick to just one paramount aim. If you do this, and get it right, the rest of the thesis will follow beautifully. If you have two aims, you will have two themes bumping along in your report together, and the reader will not be able to work out what you are doing.

- The conclusions in your last chapter must respond to this aim. Obvious? Remember Graham's thesis that the examiners sent back for rewriting and, when you have written the last sentence of your conclusions, go back and re-read your aim. If the conclusions don't respond to it, you had better rewrite it and, don't forget, you will also need to rewrite the problem statement that leads up to it.

Scope

Recall the list of questions that examiners may typically be asked to think of as they look over your thesis. One question was, 'Does the candidate show sufficient familiarity with, and understanding and critical appraisal of, the relevant literature?' You will need to think critically at each stage of your work. To start the process of being critical, you must first set limits. A major part of being critical is to be able to set the terms of your debate and focus on what is particularly relevant to achieve your aim.

Here is a little trick we use in our introductory thesis writing seminars on 'How to get started'. We ask the students to name the best restaurant in Melbourne. Very quickly they complain that this is an impossible question to answer, because it sets off the need to ask a number of related questions. Best for whom?

Under what conditions? How far away is it? What type of food? How expensive are the main dishes? You can quickly see that our simple investigation could never be completed. We then nominate a scope for our investigation (e.g., an Italian restaurant within five kilometres of the CBD that has main meals for under $20) and begin our discussion in a more focused way.

In some areas the discussion of the scope of the investigation might require only a few sentences. In others, especially newly developing areas, it might require quite an elaborate discussion.

If the terms you are going to explore in your study are especially contentious, and there are a number of these, you may need to set out a list of key definitions and put these into your first appendix. If there are only a few terms, embed these into one or two paragraphs in this section.

Also you should consider here whether you need to limit the theoretical basis of your study. Now is the time to state the criteria for the inclusion or exclusion of debated points of view, or to spell out your own biases for pursuing a certain school of thought rather than an equally valid, but different, school. You will need to justify your reasons for choosing one over the other, and that is certainly one of the hallmarks of good critical thinking. You may not be able to do this until you have developed your appraisal of the literature, in which case you might just flag the point here and take it up again when you are reviewing existing work in your next chapter.

Box 9 gives an example, from the thesis Equitable and Sustainable Development in Less Developed Countries by Jarunun Sutiprapa, of an attempt to limit the scope of a project.

> The aim of this study is to explore development policies for less developed countries within the context of the present economic system that will be both equitable and environmentally sustainable.

Box 9: An example of an attempt to limit the scope of a study

In Chapter 2 of her thesis Jarunun discussed the way that development policies had changed over the past fifty years in response to perceived problems and shortcomings in development programs. She was aware that among the development theorists there was a body of thinkers who rejected the whole notion of 'development' as understood at present, and who advocated a new 'grassroots' approach to it that operated outside the confines of conventional economics. However, if she had followed this line of thought it would have taken her project on a different path from the one she wished to follow. So she stated a limitation of the scope of her work by including the words 'within the context of the present economic system' within her aim.

The way she dealt with this seemed adequate to me at the time, but in retrospect I should have suggested that she omit this clause from her aim and instead start a separate paragraph which limited the scope of her study. This would have enabled her to not only state the constraint: she could also tell the examiner that she was aware of this alternative approach to development and why she was not considering it in her study.

If you set out your limits, you are more likely to finish the thesis; your supervisor will know what you are interested in and resist attempts to send you further afield; your examiners will be impressed that they have in hand a very focused study; and, most importantly, it will help you to produce a much more critical tone throughout your writing.

Overview of the study

The overview of the study should follow on logically from your statement of the aim. You should be able to start it off by saying, 'To achieve the above aim, Chapter 2 does ... etc.' In other words, it is a slightly expanded version of the table of contents. However, rather than writing it as a list of chapter and section headings, you should write it in the form of interconnected sentences and paragraphs to ensure that the logic flow is clear to the reader. Box 10 gives an example, taken from the PhD thesis of Srisuda Jarayabhand, Management of Coastal Aquaculture in Thailand.

In Chapter 1 of her PhD thesis Management of Coastal Aquaculture in Thailand, Srisuda Jarayabhand gives the following overview of her thesis:

The first two chapters examine the literature on the aquaculture industry in Thailand. Chapter 2 looks at the unsustainable pattern of aquaculture development happening in Thailand at present. It points out the problems and also argues the need for a sustainable approach to aquaculture. Lastly, the chapter explores existing approaches to sustainable aquaculture development. Chapter 3 examines the need to take into consideration the concept of coastal zone management in Thailand, and demonstrates its importance as an integrated approach to deal with various development activities occurring in the coastal zone.

Based on Chapters 2 and 3, Chapter 4 develops an appropriate research method for constructing a site suitability assessment model for aquaculture development. It highlights the need for spatial decision-making in managing coastal aquaculture. Chapter 5 selects a suitable study area in which the research method can be developed and tested. Chapters 6 and 7 develop the two sub-models identified in Chapter 4. The first sub-model, which will be described in Chapter 6, involves the application of Geographic Information Systems (GIS) to assist in assessment of the suitability of sites for aquaculture. Chapter 7 deals with the second sub-model, which is assessment of the capacity of the coastal ecosystem to absorb wastes from aquaculture. Finally, the results from the two sub-models are integrated to permit identification of the options for sustainable aquaculture. The model is evaluated in Chapter 8, and conclusions are drawn in Chapter 9.

Box 10: A typical section on 'Overview of the study'

An examiner who read this would have a clear idea of not only how the thesis was going to develop, but also of how the various parts of it relate to each other.

We suggest you call this section 'Overview of the study', rather than 'Method' or 'Research approach', even though it describes the method that you will use for your whole research project. The difficulty is that most people use the word *method* to describe the method used in that part of the total research program that they have designed themselves—their own surveys, interviews, observations, analyses, experiments etc. They then often give Chapter 4 or 5, which introduces this research program within a research program, the heading 'Method'. The point is that you are in danger of using the word in two senses: the method used to develop the whole of the report or thesis, and the method used for that part of the research program that you designed yourself (which we labelled *own work* in Figure 1). You must decide in which sense you will use it. We recommend that you reserve it for the method used in that part of the work designed by you, the researcher, and to use *overview of the study* to describe the approach used in the whole project—which will include historical reviews, reviews of theory and practice, accounts of the researcher's own work, and synthesis of all of these to permit conclusions to be drawn.

Revising as you work

It is necessary to revise this introductory chapter as you make new discoveries in your work. Almost imperceptibly, your aim can change as you go along, or your work may no longer lie within the scope you first established. When I (Paul Gruba) wrote my thesis The Role of Digital Video Media in Second Language Listening Comprehension, the first draft of my introductory chapter was essentially a summary of my first go at understanding the literature. It turned out to be over twenty pages. (Later, I followed David's advice and brought it down to a much more focused and manageable seven pages.) The draft included a promise that I would discuss the implications of my work for how teachers teach. But my research became much more theoretical than I had originally planned: I did not deal with its practical uses. And I had forgotten to revise my introductory chapter. The examiners then wondered why I had not talked about the pedagogical aspects of my research. When I rewrote the first chapter for final submission, the first thing I did was to delete that promise to cover the use of my work for classroom teachers!

Many students resist writing the introduction early in the project because they suspect that its direction is likely to shift as they go along, as mine did. Don't let this stop you. Write the introductory chapter as confidently as you can when you first start out. In this first draft you may not be able to limit the scope of your study sufficiently, and almost certainly you will be a bit tentative in your aim. But you will have made a start. As you come to grips with the complexity of your research, revisit the introductory chapter periodically and make any minor changes necessary. When you read it, ask yourself, are you still trying to achieve that *particular* single aim? Is the scope the one you began with? Look, too, at your working title: does it still describe what you are doing? Have a good look at your introductory chapter at regular intervals, say every three months, and certainly whenever you complete another chapter.

Stay aware when you change direction (it will happen!) and revise your introductory chapter to take account of those changes. If you do this, you will avoid the problem that caused Graham so much trouble. Remember, although you wrote the thesis over a period of years, your examiners will read it over a period of a few days, and any discrepancies between the aim, the content and the conclusions will be very obvious to them.

SUMMARY

Your introductory chapter should consist of three sections:

Problem statement (or background to the study)

- Tell the reader why you are doing the research.
- Refer to the literature only to the extent needed to demonstrate why your project is worth doing. Reserve your full review of existing theory or practice for later chapters.
- Make sure that your account of why you are doing the research leads logically to your aim.

Aim and scope

- Make sure that your aim responds to the problem statement.
- Stick rigorously to a single aim. Do not include elements in it that describe how you intend to achieve this aim. Reserve these for a later chapter.
- When you have written the conclusions to your whole study, check that they respond to this aim. If they don't, change the aim or rethink your conclusions.
- If you change the aim, you will also have to change the problem statement that leads up to it.
- Make sure that you establish the limits of your study.

Overview of the study (or structure of the thesis)

- Sketch out how the thesis is structured. Don't confine yourself to a list of the chapters, but show how they are logically interlinked.
- Check whether the reader will be able to see from this sketch how the aim will be achieved

Revising your introduction

- To avoid making promises to the examiner that you don't keep, look over your introductory chapter on a regular basis, and revise it accordingly.

6 The background chapters

Depending on the nature of the report, the background chapter or chapters may take many different forms. However, their function is always the same: to provide the context for your own work.

The three most common types of background chapter are:

- *Descriptive material* to locate study areas in space, time or culture;
- *Reviews of existing theory or practice;*
- *Preliminary investigations or surveys* done by you or others that will help to formulate hypotheses for the major research program to follow.

You may have one or more of these, depending on the type of research you are doing. For example, if you were reporting on strategies to control the environmental impact of human activities on Antarctica, you would certainly need a descriptive chapter on the Antarctic climate and landform. You would also have a chapter reviewing the development of human activities there, together with the impacts of these activities (current practice). You might also include another chapter reviewing the theory of the control of environmental impacts (existing theory). These background chapters would provide the basis for your own work, which might include surveys to establish likely future problems, and critical thinking about how such future problems might best be contained.

Getting started on the background chapters

Within the first few months of your candidature your supervisor will doubtless suggest that you do some writing to get your research going. Depending on your project, this will most likely be material in the first two categories above:

- Historical, geographical or other types of description of your study area. Reviews of existing practice in the field of research are a type of descriptive chapter;
- Reviews of theories or ideas about your research topic developed by other researchers.

Assuming your topic does not change greatly over the next year or so, it will be possible to incorporate bits of this writing in some appropriate form in your background chapters. As we urged in Chapter 3, you should try to see these preliminary writings as if they were going to form part of your final thesis. They should be written in a scholarly mode, including proper referencing to the work or ideas of previous workers in this field, and when you write them you should use the template that you intend to use for your final thesis. This is quite straight-forward, and easy to do, providing you are determined to set off on the right foot, and spend a little time learning how to use the styles, templates and the scholarly conventions of your field. You will have to do this anyway in the end, so why not start now?

You should also be asking yourself, 'What do I want this material to lead to?'. This is more difficult, because you know less now about your topic than you will when you eventually complete your project and write it up in the form of a thesis. Nevertheless, it is worth trying to do, for two reasons: (a) It is a good habit of mind to always ask yourself what you are trying to achieve before you start writing; (b) It may prevent you from writing a lot of unnecessary material that you will later have to throw away.

Descriptive material

Tony McDonald was writing a research report on the usefulness of laser grading of irrigated farmland. In this process laser-guided machinery is used to grade the land extremely precisely, so that the irrigation water will flow evenly over the whole of the land. In this way the depth of flooding required to ensure that the whole area is properly irrigated is reduced, and no areas are left waterlogged. These good effects may be counter-balanced by alterations to plant growth caused by disturbance to the soil by the grading operation, for example through loss of soil nutrients and bacteria. To understand all of these effects, the reader needs a description of the interaction between soil, water, plants and air. How much of this should Tony have included as a background chapter? At first he left it all out, assuming the reader would know as much about this as he did. I, his supervisor, didn't, and told him that he would have to include enough of this material so that the policy maker, as distinct from the agricultural scientist, would be able to understand what he was talking about. A week or so later I asked how his description of the soil and plants was going, and he told me that he had written about thirty pages and was only half way through. He was busily paraphrasing from half a dozen standard soil texts and distilling the thoughts of the three soil scientists he had previously interviewed! What he should have been doing (and eventually did) was something between these two extremes.

What tests should you apply to find out what to omit from a descriptive chapter and what to include? We suggest two:

- Only include material that the reader needs in order to understand what will follow. Although we need some soil science to understand the effects of laser grading on the soil, there is a lot that is not relevant to the problem.

- Don't include anything in your main text if it is going to interrupt the development of your logic. Text of this sort may have to be included in the thesis, but belongs in appendixes.*

Reviews of theory

The old approach to thesis writing required students to produce a chapter entitled 'Literature review', all formally typed up, before they were permitted to proceed with their own work. The idea was that this review would help them to see just where previous workers had drawn unwarranted conclusions or had disagreed with each other. The students would then be able to design brilliant experiments to resolve these problems.

You should certainly read the literature before you leap into a full-scale research program, and attempt to write a report describing your understanding of it. This is the only way you can learn how to follow the important arguments through. But until you have done some work of your own it will not be possible to be 'critical' in the sense implied by 'a critical review of the literature'. It follows that you will not yet be able to design those brilliant experiments that have so far eluded all the skilled researchers in the area. You will be able to design a research program, but almost certainly it will be tentative. With luck, the results of this preliminary program may help you to design a better set of surveys or experiments next time (by now you will have thought about it a bit more, and will have gone back and re-read the literature). Your reviewing of the literature will be

---

* *Appendixes* or *appendices*? *Appendix* is a Latin word whose Latin plural is *appendices*. The modern trend to anglicize foreign plurals has caught up with *appendix*, and the Oxford dictionary now gives *appendixes* as a permitted plural. Please yourself—but be consistent.

an ongoing process: you will probably still be reading it when you are writing your conclusions.

How do you convert your initial 'literature survey' into a critical review of existing theory that will lead logically into the work that you design and undertake yourself? A review of current theory has three functions:

- It gives the background information required to contextualize the extent and significance of your research problem;
- It identifies and discusses attempts by others to solve similar problems; and
- It provides examples of methods they have employed in attempts to solve these problems.

Make sure you deal with all of these.

The first function is the most straightforward. Its sole purpose is to establish the parameters of your argument. Guide yourself through this section of the research by asking the journalist's four standard questions: Who? What? Where? and When? Keep this section short, and do not get caught up in unnecessary detail. Simply put, it provides a map of the territory you are seeking to cover. It signals to your readers that you intend to follow the scope of your investigation and are confident enough to guide them through the complexities of the topic.

First attempts to review existing theory often stop at this point. But when you have put your problem in the context of current research in the area you have hardly started! Identifying and discussing the approach of other researchers to your problem is the second function of your review. This is where you will need those critical skills. It is likely (and expected) that you will have read much more widely in the topic area than you will need for your review. Your initial journey through the literature will have helped you gain a better understanding of the many facets of your central problem, but you will not need not to deal with all of them in full. Keep in mind the aim and scope of your thesis: How does what you are reading relate to achieving your stated aim?

As you read, write: the act of writing itself will force you to come to grips with conflicting ideas and focus your attention on the most important arguments. You will gain a sense of what parts of the previous research are leading you towards possible ways of dealing with your problem. As you develop a stronger sense of the field, constantly strive to filter the good from the bad. What you are doing at this point is creating an internal set of criteria on which to accept or reject arguments and, through this process, you will develop the ability to think critically. By now you will probably have written many fragments and mini-reviews, and it is time to write a proper first draft of your 'critical review of existing theory'. Before you hand this to your supervisor, it's a good idea to put it aside for a week or so and work on something else. Then come back to it and try to rework it as though you were reading it through the examiners' eyes. In this second draft, try to articulate the criteria you have been using to accept or reject arguments and to demonstrate to readers just how sharp your criticisms are.

From your previous reading and your attendance at research seminars in your department you will probably have become aware of the flaws in research design, research methods and the reporting of results that can mar an otherwise competent investigation. Seek out the advice of specialists who provide lists of common methodological mistakes and general advice on how to proceed.

Once you get to know some of the common mistakes, stay alert to them as you review previous studies. Use that knowledge to point out how a previous investigation may have made only a limited contribution to solving your problem. (If the contribution had not been limited, you would not have to conduct an investigation—somebody else has already solved the problem!) But remember also to point out how these other studies may have advanced the discipline. If it has been published, it must have made some sort of contribution. Summarize these contributions completely and honestly. Examiners will be sensitive to instances in which major contributions are neglected, or their significance downplayed.

Throughout this second section of your review, keep in mind that you are 'engaging in a conversation' with other academics. Engagement is the key concept: it means you are ready, in a spirit of 'give and take', to respect the value of multiple perspectives. It is easy to make the mistake of thinking that the function of this section is merely to 'report' or 'describe' previous studies in an effort to show that you have 'done your homework'. Rather, interweave various studies to build up the argument that the problem you are tackling is not yet solved and still raises some complex (and unanswered) questions.

Eventually, you will come to an understanding of the most recent thinking in the field. At that point, briefly summarize the main points that await research. You have identified the 'gaps' in the theoretical framework and areas that remain relatively unexplored by previous researchers. This summary should set the ground for the questions or hypotheses that you will identify in your chapter on the design of your own research. These are the gaps that you will be trying to fill with your own work.

In the final part of your review you should examine the approaches others used in trying to solve the problem and, where appropriate, point out the limitations to those approaches. (Remember, one of the attributes of a PhD thesis is that it is aware of limitations—see the second point in Box 1 in Chapter 2.) No method is 'perfect', but your review should lead to an understanding of which methods can be used to achieve solutions to your problem. You will draw on this in your next chapter, where you select appropriate methods for your own research program.

Preliminary investigations

Peter came to me in some puzzlement, announcing that his experiments had failed. He was investigating a problem in the utilization of brown coal, and had designed some preliminary experiments based on hypotheses drawn from overseas work in the same field using German brown coals. What he expected to happen had not happened, and what had happened was quite unexpected. His 'experiments had failed'. I assured him that they had succeeded, not failed. He had been lucky enough to have the unexpected happen, under conditions where he was sure it *had* happened, because he was making careful observations. If he could work out *why* it might have happened, he would have far better hypotheses than when he was depending solely on the German literature.

Most research workers when tackling a new project will use a variety of methods. As you can see from the example of Peter's work, it can be difficult to establish from the literature alone what experimental work you should do, because you are an outsider listening to a debate. If you are to take part in that debate you will need to have some practical experience of your own. In the physical or biological sciences this might consist of designing some simple experiments to enable you to test the results or theories of earlier workers, as Peter had done. In the social sciences some preliminary surveys or interviews could be useful. Extracting published data of a number of different workers and trying to fit them to a popular theoretical model is another method.

Where should an account of this preliminary work appear in your thesis? If you have used it to help you to formulate hypotheses that you have called on when designing your principal research program, you could report the preliminary work as one of the background chapters. If it appears to form a major element of the principal work itself, you should set it aside for reporting later as part of the 'Design' and 'Results' chapters. If you report preliminary investigations in a background chapter, it will have to contain sections on the hypothesis used, the design of the work, the results and the conclusions drawn from them. In either case, be sure that you make clear the need for its inclusion—you don't want to appear as if you are trying to 'pad out' your work by putting in somewhat irrelevant material.

Revising

As we have recommended earlier, there is much to be gained in writing the background chapters before or during the time when you are carrying out your own research program. However, when you have finished your own research it is time to rewrite the background chapters. You are now much clearer about several things than you were when you first wrote them:

• You are now clearer about the links between your own work and the work of others who went before you;
• You now know what assumptions you made, quite unconsciously, about your study area. These can now be made explicit;
• You are aware of the issues surrounding the application of current methods in your field, and have explicitly pointed out their limitations;
• You will have realized (perhaps with the help of feedback from your supervisors and participants in your research seminars) that you were making unwarranted assumptions about the level of knowledge of other people about the background to your own work. For example, if you come from India and your project is located in India, you might assume that the reader was as familiar with the names of all the states of India as you are. What if one of your examiners comes from Finland?
• In your efforts to understand and interpret the results of your own work you will have reached a new level of understanding of the work of others—this is what is meant by a 'critical' understanding. For example, if you were working in the area of 'Sustainable Architecture', you would by now have realized that many people writing about it had been using

the words as a vague catchphrase, and you will have to go back and make some very careful definitions about it.

- Most likely you designed your own work without being completely conscious of the research questions or even the hypotheses that informed it. This probably sounds silly, but our experience with most students is that this is what happens. When we ask students why they did something and they have no ready answer they sometimes get quite a shock. This does not mean that the work does not have a valid basis, but rather that the driving force behind it was in part developed in the unconscious mind. It now has to be made conscious. In your research design chapter (see Chapter 7) you will have to make it conscious, and your background chapters will have to lead into the research questions or hypotheses that you announce in your research design chapter.

This gives us some guidelines on how you should tackle the revising of the background chapters:

- You must ensure that the ways that you are going to use words and ideas are carefully defined. Where these are fundamental to your own work, the development of these ideas in the literature or even in the history of ideas must be discussed. For example, in her thesis on Assessment of Landscape Heritage Jan Schapper had to trace through the development of the notions of heritage and landscape. Both of these words have a host of everyday meanings, but it was fundamental to her research that the reader understood precisely how she was using the terms.
- Any formal literature review that you do before you begin your own work should not appear in the final thesis in that form. What you should have, rather, is a structured account of theory current at the time you did your own work. You will be able to impose a structure on it, because by now you have finished your own work, which will have gone further than the work of others (that's why you were doing the research). You will write it with the critical perception of the

worker who has now gone past this point. The story in Chapter 3 about Len's work is a good example. He couldn't get started on his review of existing theory because he felt he had to describe the work appearing in 120 different papers. When he structured it around the ideas of the four workers who had made really significant advances in the field it was quite easy to write. You should also ensure that the structure provides a firm base for the discussion of your own work (see Chapter 9).

- How did you formulate the research questions or hypotheses that you used to help you to design your own research program? When students present us with a proposed work program and we ask what it is based on, they often reply that it is obvious, or that it just came to them. These responses are both true from where they stand, but will not convince examiners. They will have to be argued out. We touched on this problem in Chapter 3, 'Making a Strong Start'. What apparently happens is that our unconscious mind works on various fragments of ideas from different sources that come to us from our reading and our senses, and makes connections that our rational mind will not. These connections emerge not as new rational thoughts but rather as proposals for action. We then implement these proposals in the form of research designs without actually making the underlying logic of them explicit as research questions or hypotheses. If this happened for you, you now have to work your way backwards from your research program to why you did it the way you did, i.e. what your research questions or hypotheses were. You then have to work your way back further to where these questions or hypotheses came from, and ensure that at the very least the conclusions of your background chapters prepared the way for them. You will then have to make sure that the appropriate material is present in the background chapters to enable these conclusions to be drawn.

- You will have to be ready to cut material out of background chapters if it is not used elsewhere in the thesis. The background chapters are not ends in themselves. They are merely the context for your own work. We have already mentioned some tests for what to include and what not to include in descriptive chapters. Be ruthless! If you are not making use of material either as background to your own work or as context for the discussion of your results, chop it out! A survey of literature on a topic unrelated to your own work will not please an examiner looking for critical thinking.

- Finally, there is another type of material that you should remove. Because students know what they found out themselves they sometimes forget that the examiner does not know. Remove all material from background chapters that is to do with the design of your own work, the results of your own work, or the discussion of these results. Don't puzzle the examiner, and at the same time steal your own thunder!

SUMMARY

The background chapters have the following functions:

To provide all the background material needed for your own research:

- Historical, geographical and other descriptions of your study area.
- Definitions and usages of words and expressions as you will use them in the thesis.
- Existing theory about your research topic
- Existing practice about your research topic.
- In some cases, preliminary reviews, surveys, correlations and even experiments following what other workers have done.

To provide the stepping-off point for your own research:

- The conclusions to these chapters should lead clearly to the research hypotheses or research questions that you identify in your research design chapter (see Chapter 7).

How to write them

- Write first drafts of them within the first year of your project. Don't forget to use the formatting, referencing etc. that you intend to use in the final thesis (see Chapter 4).
- Many researchers, particularly in the experimental sciences, put this writing off until they have finished their research. Don't delay. Writing early drafts will help to sharpen up your research design.
- These first drafts will probably not be well structured, as you are not yet on top of your topic. You must be prepared to restructure them later, after you have done most of your own work. This double handling is not a waste of time, as it will make a fruitful contribution to your own research.
- When you rewrite them, check that the conclusions do lead into your research questions or hypotheses. If they don't, it probably shows that your original structure left out critical material that will now have to be added.

What you should include in them

- All necessary definitions and ways that you will use words or ideas in your own work. Don't just assume that the examiner will know this. This is particularly important in cross-disciplinary research.
- All the necessary geography and history. Would a Finnish examiner be familiar with all the States of India?
- All the arguments that have been going on in the literature, and some tentative judgement on where you stand on them (but don't enter the argument yet; wait till you have described your own work).
- Everything necessary to justify the conclusions to the chapters, which in turn have to lead to your research hypotheses or questions in your research design chapter.

What you should not include

- Descriptive material that will never be used later in the thesis. Your first draft will probably contain a lot of this. Be ruthless: chop it out!

- Your own contribution to the theory. By the time you come to revise these chapters you should be in a position to make such contributions. Resist the temptation. Save these contributions for your discussion chapter.
- Any foreshadowing of what you will be doing in your own research. You can't do this until you have designed your own research, and you can't do that until you have finished all these chapters. Don't get ahead of yourself.

7 The chapter on design of your own work

Vineeta Hoon had spent the best part of a year with the Bhotiya people of the Himalayas. These people spend their winters in villages in the foothills of the mountains, and their summers in villages in the mountains themselves, growing crops and grazing their sheep in the mountain valleys. The aim of her project was, roughly, to find whether the Bhotiya society could survive in modern India. When she began it, nobody could even tell her whether this society still did survive: the literature describing it had been written fifty or more years earlier.

She was told to head north, and try to find them! She did, equipped with the research techniques of the human geographer, and carrying with her warm clothes and useful instruments for measuring, weighing and recording. What was she going to do, if and when she found them? Live with them in their winter villages in the foothills; go on the month-long trek to the summer villages; live with them there, observe them, talk with them, note what they did in their everyday activities, who took part in each activity, how long each took, what quantities of food and fuel they used, where it came from, and so on.

Some time after she finished this work, she came to Australia for a year as a guest of the Australian Federation of University

Women, with the intention of writing her PhD thesis on Himalayan Transhumance and Nomadism. That's how she came to knock on my door. Could I help her analyse the energy flows involved in Bhotiya farming? I could. I ended up supervising the writing of her whole thesis.

Her work illustrates, in an extreme form, the problem of research design. She seemed to have virtually no control over her 'experiments'; her subjects were just people going about their daily lives. What would she measure? What would she talk to them about? What mattered and what didn't, in terms of fulfilling her research aim? The physical scientist would be appalled at her inability to carry out those 'crucial experiments' always mentioned in accounts of the scientific method. Even many social scientists might be bothered by her inability to select representative subjects, and the difficulty of formulating and testing hypotheses about their thought and actions. Does this mean that she was just thrashing around blindly in her year with them, recording scraps of information at random, and was now faced with the task of making sense of these random observations, not to mention the even more difficult task of demonstrating to her examiners that she knew what she was doing?*

Your own work may be a long way in concept from Vineeta's. But even if it is the hardest of 'hard science', you will have the same problem as she did. You have to describe why you did what you did. By the time you start to describe your results (in the 'Results' chapter(s) you will be so immersed in them that you may have quite forgotten the struggle you went through to

---

* Of course, she had set out with quite a clear idea of the research instruments she would use. In the field she had to adapt these instruments to the circumstances she found herself in. What she had to explain to the examiners was why these were suitable instruments, and why they had to be adapted. Her study has now been published as a book, *Living on the Move*.

select an appropriate method for your investigations, or why you designed your research instruments as you did.* As a result, it is quite easy to jump straight from your background chapters to your results, with only a very brief section in the 'Results' chapter to cover these points. This could leave your reader mystified as to your reasoning, and thus make the results of your investigations difficult to follow. The examiner's task is to pass you if you show that you know what you are doing, and to fail you if you don't.

Your account of the design of your own investigations is the place where this virtue or failing is most obvious. What you say will depend on the type of research you are engaged in and the research methods that you have used. When designing the research, you will have used your preliminary reading and investigations to generate hypotheses or throw up research questions. Now you must identify these hypotheses or research questions and argue for them. If you have done your research properly you will have selected, from the range available, a research method or methods appropriate for testing your hypotheses or answering your questions. In your report or thesis you should review the methods available and tell your reader why you chose your particular method or methods of investigation. Finally, you will report on the specific design of the research instruments. If your chosen method involves using a case study, you will need to spend some time saying why you decided to use the case-study approach. You will also need to say why you chose that particular case study, and spend some time describing it. (If an elaborate description is needed, you may find it desirable to put this in a separate chapter after your research design chapter,

---

* We shall use the term 'research instruments' in this chapter to include all the techniques that physical and social scientists might use to carry out their 'own work', including, for example, controlled experiments, surveys of various kinds, interviews of various kinds, unobtrusive observation, participant observation, and content analysis.

but don't fall into the trap of making this description one of your background chapters. You can't describe your case study before you have selected it. If you try to do this you will have trouble explaining to the reader why you are doing so.)

Generation of hypotheses

Thomas came to me wishing to do a PhD. When I asked him what the aim of his project was, he replied that it was to demonstrate that development in his home country, one of the African nations, depended crucially on the adequate provision of household energy supplies. This is a hypothesis, not an aim. (An aim here might be to investigate the relationship between national development and the availability of household energy supplies.) This confusion is very common. More often than not, when I ask potential research students what the aim of their research is, they reply with a hypothesis. The confusion seems to be due to a looseness of expression amongst research workers when talking about research. As we discussed in Chapter 3, research is a complex mixture of creative and rational processes. As a result, it is quite common to leap right into the middle of the research process with a hypothesis, and work backwards to the aim and forwards to the conclusions at the same time.* But it doesn't do to assume you know the answer before you start— you'll remember from the previous chapter Peter's conclusion that his 'experiments had failed'.

However, no matter how irrational and chancy the research is, the report of it must be argued logically and clearly. Therefore you must eliminate any confusion between *aim* and *hypothesis*. *Aim* is to do with directing something towards an object, whereas a *hypothesis* is a proposition made as a starting point for further

---

* If that sounds confusing, it is because the research process *is* confusing. Read about it in Arthur Koestler's book, *The Sleepwalkers*.

investigation from known facts.* Clearly the two words have quite different meanings, and should not be used interchangeably.

To be fair to my potential students, they were not really confusing the two things. They *were* giving me hypotheses: propositions that could be tested. They had perceived problems, and had developed hypotheses about them in their unconscious thoughts over a period of time, long before they had come to me to start their PhD projects. When they came to see me they had not yet worked their way back from their hypotheses to their aims. They were thinking about what they could *do* in their research, rather than what they were trying to *achieve*. When I asked about their aims, perhaps not surprisingly they gave me their hypotheses.

When I explain the difference, referring to the dictionary if necessary, students often reply that their aim is to 'prove' their hypothesis. This is not an aim either! Testing, so that we can uphold or refute our hypothesis, is what we *do* to hypotheses. A hypothesis is just a device for enabling us to set up useful tests or experiments that will tell us whether we are on the right track in our quest. It is not the arrow pointing to the destination.

It follows that you should not use the word 'hypothesis' in the opening chapter of your thesis. In a recent seminar a student told me that her supervisor said the first chapter of a thesis should be an extensive review of the literature ending up with a research hypothesis, which seems to cut across the above

---

* G. W. Turner (ed.), *The Australian Concise Oxford Dictionary.* Consider an archer: her aim is to put the arrow in the bull's-eye. She might have a hypothesis that if she was shooting in a northerly direction and the wind was blowing from the east at 10 metres per second she would have to shoot at a point 2 degrees to the right of the bull's-eye. She could quite easily test this hypothesis by shooting a group of arrows at the bull's-eye and another group 2 degrees to the right When she had tested her hypothesis she would be in a better position to achieve her original aim, which was to get arrows in the bull's-eye.

advice. However, as we pointed out in Chapter 3, what he was really advocating, without realizing it, was omitting the first chapter of the thesis altogether. This is dangerous! If you do this you will inevitably get the aim and the hypothesis mixed up, and may never identify the aim of your project clearly. Your first mention of the word hypothesis should be in the chapter we are now discussing. When you do use it, stick strictly to its formal meaning. You should be able to deduce from the combination of your reading and your preliminary work that there are certain lines of thought worth following up, or worth testing by careful tests. These tests are the ones that, in the classical 'scientific method', are called crucial experiments. They will tell you without doubt whether your hypothesis has stood up or whether it has been demolished. Either way you have made progress.

Therefore, in the first section after the introduction to this chapter you should identify the ideas emerging from your background chapters that are worth following up in your own work. Whether you identify them rigorously as hypotheses for testing or as questions to be answered will depend on the type of research you are doing. But whichever you use you should develop them clearly and strongly, strongly enough for you to be able to select appropriate methods for testing them or following them up.

Selection of method

If you examine a range of theses from the library you will probably see that in many of them the chapter we are discussing is titled 'Method' or 'Research method'. You may also see 'Methodology' or 'Research methodology'. We have suggested instead that this chapter should be titled 'Research design' because, as we have just seen, it includes more than the selection and description of your method. It should start with a drawing together of reviews of previous work and preliminary studies to formulate research hypotheses or research questions. The methods we select are ways of testing the hypotheses or answering the questions. Therefore, if you call the chapter 'Research method', you are in danger of forgetting to deal adequately with the identification of hypotheses or questions.

In passing, we have just touched on another problem, the distinction between *method* and *methodology*. Often researchers in the sciences use the word 'methodology' when they mean 'method', perhaps because it sounds more learned. However, as any dictionary will show, methodology is the branch of knowledge that deals with method and its application in a particular field of study: methodology comes before method. For this reason social scientists use the word methodology to indicate how we gain knowledge of the world, i.e. the general stance that the researcher is taking, for example the researcher as the designer of empirical experiments, the researcher as objective observer, or the researcher as participant in the activities under study.* You should reserve it for this usage, and should not use it to describe the design of empirical experiments or objective observations of physical or biological systems. When scientists are designing work of this kind they probably do not realize that they are taking a particular stance, the researcher as dispassionate outsider, and don't see any need to discuss their methodology.

However, in many areas of social sciences and humanities it is important to tell the reader what stance you are taking, and why. This should be discussed in a separate section on methodology. In this section, you should consider identifying your stance on the information or data that you will be analysing. Do you believe, for example, that your findings are best viewed from a neo-Marxist or post-modernist perspective? Are you undertaking to construct a 'feminist reading' of the incidents that you have witnessed? Will your analysis be coloured by a 'liberal' or a 'labour' understanding of the political landscape? If you

---

* See, for example, Denzin and Lincoln (eds), *Handbook of Qualitative Research*, pp. 99–100.

do take a particular philosophical stance towards your study, our advice here is that you make it clear to the reader that it was from this stance that you chose which 'method' to use to gather data. Justify why you decided to use such a perspective from among the many competing viewpoints, and how that perspective informs your choice of data collection methods or instruments. Later, of course, you will need to refer to this perspective as you analyse your data and discuss your findings.

Now you must tell your readers what method or methods you used to test your hypotheses or answer your questions, and why you chose them. You should first review the methods available to you, and then present reasons for selecting the methods you used. It is easy to forget this step altogether when writing your thesis. You may have used a fairly standard method used by your predecessors for testing the type of hypothesis you have put forward. You may have adopted a method suggested by colleagues or supervisors as being suitable. In both these cases you would scarcely be aware that you had *selected* a method. Or, as we suggested earlier, you might have put a lot of thought into the selection of your method, but by the time you came to report the results, you were so immersed in them that you completely overlooked the need to say why you chose that particular method.

But the reader cannot read your mind. No examiner is going to be kind enough to say, 'Well I expect the candidate had good reasons for selecting that particular method'. If you turn back to question 3 in Box 2 in Chapter 2, you will see that in the University of Melbourne examiners are specifically asked to check whether the methods you have adopted are appropriate, and whether you have justified your selection of them.

Using multiple methods or perspectives

Surveyors faced with the problem of locating the position of a distant inaccessible point can tackle this problem by measuring the lengths and angles of two accessible lines leading to it. To be sure that they have it right they can select another pair of lines and repeat the process, perhaps by going around the other side of the obstruction. The two locations they have identified should agree within acceptable limits. This process is called triangulation, because the surveyor is making use of the properties of triangles to make the necessary calculations. The important point is that they make two estimates of the position of the point by coming at it from different directions.

The term triangulation is used in research work by analogy when we use more than one research method or type of data to answer our research questions or test our hypotheses.* We might do this if we had more than one hypothesis or question, or if the question was multi-faceted, and different methods or different approaches of the investigator were needed to throw light on the different facets. This is quite common in research in the social sciences. For example, in her study of the Bhotiyas Vineeta Hoon used both time analysis and space analysis of their activities. She also used energy analysis to determine whether their activities were sustainable, and she supplemented all of this by the use of focused interviews and participant observation. In the experimental sciences it is quite common to supplement empirical observation of a complex system by calculating the expected behaviour of the system using a mathematical model. Geoff Thomas used this approach in his study of the ignition of coal particles mentioned in Chapter 5.

If you use more than one method or approach, you not only have to describe each of the them and why you selected them, but also why one was not enough.

---

* Triangulation is used in different ways in different kinds of research: data triangulation, investigator triangulation, theory triangulation, and methodological triangulation. For a fuller discussion of triangulation in research, see Denzin and Lincoln (eds), *Handbook of Qualitative Research*, pp. 214–15.

Study or case study?

Particular phenomena can be studied in their own right or to provide information on a broad range of similar phenomena. For example, we might study the seeding, germination and growth of the river red gum, *Eucalyptus camaldulensis,* because we wish to know how to control its environment to ensure its viability. Alternatively, we might be studying this particular species because we recognize it as being representative of a whole range of river-bank flora. If we found its development to be sensitive to the pattern of river levels over a few seasons (as indeed it is), we might then be bold enough to generalize, and suggest that this sensitivity could be expected in other riparian flora. In the second case, we have used the study of *E. camaldulensis* as a 'case study',* and the outcome of our study is a theory on the life cycle of riparian flora.

Thus, using a case-study approach is essentially a way to build theory. In your review of current theory, for example, you might have identified gaps in the understanding of something in your area and are now seeking to fill these gaps. Your 'statement of the problem' may revolve around strengthening a conceptual definition, challenging an existing way of thinking or examining patterns in feminist thinking across the last twenty years. You are not focusing on a specific instance or a particular author but rather are seeking a way to argue your point within an overall conceptual framework.

The aim and content of your thesis will be quite different for the two approaches. Therefore, you must be clear whether you are investigating a phenomenon *in its own right* or as a *case study* from which you might later draw some generalizations.

In the social sciences the use of case studies is very common. So is confusion about how to deal with them in theses. Let me

---

* See Yin, *Case Study Research: Design and Methods,* for a fuller account of the uses and execution of case study work.

give you an example. Emma Wakeham selected the topic 'Managing the Victoria Hill Mine Site in Bendigo' for her honours research report.* This is the site of a worked-out gold mine in the heart of Bendigo—a provincial town of some 50 000 people in the State of Victoria. This old mine site presents problems and opportunities: problems of safety and planning blight, and opportunities for preserving something of Victoria's mining heritage, perhaps combining this with tourism.

Emma's original intention was to investigate the management problems and opportunities in much the same way as a consultant might: to work through them in the light of existing legislation and land-use controls, and present a management plan. As her work continued, it became clear that the Victoria Hill mine site was not unique. Similar problems and opportunities were present in other mine sites, and her conclusions might be applicable to them also. Emma had slipped into considering Victoria Hill as a case study that could help her in a broader study of how to manage worked-out mines, rather than a study of how to manage Victoria Hill itself.

This almost imperceptible shift during a research project is quite common. Usually the research method doesn't have to change much, at least in the early stages, to adapt to the shift, but the report of the work must be quite different. The danger is that, because the shift *is* imperceptible, the researcher might fail to change the aim and content of the thesis. In Figure 4 I illustrate the differences in reporting required for these two approaches, using the Victoria Hill study as an example. I wrote these two outlines without doing the research. Had I done it, I am sure that they would have been modified and improved. However, I think that the principal elements and sequencing would have been much the same.

---

* For reasons that will become apparent, her report was eventually given a quite different title, The Mining Heritage Landscape: Our Cultural Past, Present and Future.

Study of Victoria Hill alone	Victoria Hill as a case study
Title: Managing the Victoria Hill Mine Site	**Title:** The Mining Heritage Landscape: Our Cultural Past, Present and Future
Aim: To develop a management plan for the Victoria Hill mine site in Bendigo.	**Aim:** To develop principles for managing worked-out mine sites close to urban areas.
Background: Describe Victoria Hill mine site. Review legislation and land-use controls, specifically as they apply to Victoria Hill.	**Background:** Review legislation and land-use controls. Review present practice in Australia and elsewhere on rehabilitation of disturbed landscapes. Review theory of industrial heritage.
Method: Hypothesis is that contributions from several disciplines will be needed. Interview professionals such as City Planner for Bendigo, landscape architects, tourism planners.	**Method:** Hypothesis is that the management problem can be generalized. Second hypothesis is that the present management of old mine sites is *ad hoc*, and that management principles don't exist. Select case-study approach for developing management principles. Select Victoria Hill as case study.
Results: List problems and opportunities at Victoria Hill.	**Results:** Describe Victoria Hill mine site. List problems and opportunities. Review present management practice. Confirm (most likely) that management principles do not exist.
Discussion: Derive and justify a management plan for Victoria Hill.	**Discussion:** Develop management principles applicable to Victoria Hill. Generalize them. Establish changes to laws and regulations required to put them into practice.
Conclusions: Summarize management plan (note that this is not really a conclusion, as this type of investigation has an outcome rather than a conclusion).	**Conclusions:** General management principles can be enunciated. They follow a particular pattern (summarized here). Present management of old mine sites is inadequate. Laws and regulations should be changed (as summarized here) to encourage implementation of principles.

Figure 4: Differing report outlines for an individual study and a case study

The two outlines are clearly very different. The common elements appear at different points. For example, the words 'Victoria Hill' are not even mentioned in the title or the aim in the case-study approach, and the description of the Victoria Hill mine area is deferred for several chapters. The case-study investigation is far more ambitious and involves far more work. Not surprisingly, the discussion and conclusions take a quite different course.

You must, then, be quite clear about which of the two approaches you are using. If you are undecided, you will jump from writing about a single site (or other entity) to writing up a case study as the thesis develops. When you finally get to the discussion you will be in a big mess. I have seen this happen often. We can offer an excellent test: if you mention the words 'case study' in your thesis, you should not be mentioning the specific area or topic of the case study in your aim or title. If you find that it keeps creeping back into the aim or title, you have not yet sorted out this problem.

Figure 4 demonstrates that there is a leap of faith in the discussion and conclusions sections of the case-study approach, in that it is assumed that the findings for the case study can be generalized. (If you don't go on to at least some generalization, then it is not a case study, but merely a study.) You will have done your best to cover this point in your method section, in which you try to choose the most representative case-study area. However, inevitably you will spend so much time developing ideas around your case-study area that you will have little time for the even more important task of seeing how far you can generalize them. This doubt can be resolved only by checking your conclusions on several other areas, either by doing further work yourself, which you may not have time to do, or by finding reports of comparable work in the literature. Therefore, most case-study investigations leave many unanswered questions and pose many hypotheses for further research.

Thus, a case study is an investigation that builds theory: you examine a representative instance (or setting, or group) as a way of seeing whether an existing theory really works, or to generate hypotheses or to examine the consequences of a decision. Your intention here is not to draw 'hard and fast' conclusions, but rather to act as an explorer who is mapping out, and suggesting, new areas of investigation. Yet in the right-hand column in Figure 4 the case study is the main investigation. This is quite valid. We have detailed knowledge of many PhD theses taken up principally by case-study investigations that have impressed the examiners. However, if you undertake a case-study, keep in mind that you will need to express the appropriate reservations about the degree to which your conclusions can be generalized, and to point out the need for further work to confirm your conclusions.

Design of research instruments or procedures

You have told the reader what research method you used and why you chose it. Before you describe the results obtained by using this method, you must first describe in detail *the way you applied the method, and why.* Two examples should help, one from the physical sciences and one from the social sciences.

Example 1

Geoff Thomas's study of the ignition of brown coal particles was mentioned in Chapter 5. His aim was to establish how brown coal particles ignite in burners in a power-station boiler fired with brown coal. His method was the use of controlled experiments. How would he design and carry out his experimental program?

Coal for power-station burners is pulverized in a hammer mill to a size range of 10–1000 microns. The pulverized coal is suspended in a stream of air or gas, mixed with the combustion air, and injected continuously into the hot flame formed by the combustion of the coal that immediately preceded it into the combustion chamber. If the coal particles do not get hot enough they will not ignite, and the flame will go out. It is difficult to work out how the particles are igniting, for two reasons. First, the ignition process occurs very rapidly. Second, it is difficult to observe individual particles, because they are travelling at great speed and are accompanied by many thousands of other particles.

To overcome these problems, Geoff decided to use a procedure that would simulate the ignition and combustion process, but in such a way that he could observe what was happening to individual particles. In his apparatus, coal particles were glued to the end of a glass fibre using a non-combustible glue, and plunged into a stream of hot gases whose composition and temperature could be controlled. As the particles ignited they became very hot, and therefore emitted light, which was detected by a light-sensitive cell. The output of this cell was recorded against time on a cathode-ray oscilloscope. In a variant of this procedure the igniting particles were photographed, using a high-speed movie camera.

You will notice that Geoff invoked no 'hypothesis' in the selection of the method beyond the somewhat fuzzy one that if he could 'capture' the ignition process for individual coal particles he would find out something useful about the ignition of a cloud of particles.

However, the detailed design of the experiments, and hence the physical design of the apparatus, required quite precise hypotheses. The literature on the ignition of coal particles suggested that important factors were the temperature and composition of the gases encountered by the fresh coal particles, the size of the particles, the type of coal, and its moisture content. Each of these formed a hypothesis: that the temperature of the gas affected the ignition process, that the moisture and oxygen content of the gas both affected the ignition process—and so on.

He selected values of these variables over a wide range, limited only by the design of the apparatus (for example, it was not possible to glue particles smaller than 100 microns to the glass fibre), and by the practical limits of what was being simulated (for example, it was pointless to test the effect of using an atmosphere of pure oxygen, as this would never be encountered in practice). He then devised a set of experiments using the many different combinations of these levels of the controlled variables. Each combination was repeated ten times, to take account of the heterogeneity in individual coal particles. The individual experiments were performed in random order, so that no bias would occur through such factors as improvement in experimental technique over time.

In his chapter on 'Experimental design' Geoff described the procedure and its limitations, the hypotheses concerning the effects of various factors, the design of experiments to test these hypotheses, and the design of apparatus to carry out these experiments.

Example 2

For his honours project in the social sciences, Gerard Mutimer decided to study the gap between knowledge and action in the recycling of household wastes. His idea was that if the reasons for the gap were known, it would help municipal councils to devise better recycling programs. This is a typical case of starting off with a hypothesis—that there was a gap. Clearly his project would be in great trouble if he did not test this hypothesis. Equally clearly, the testing of this hypothesis was not the aim of the project, but a step in the method.

As Gerard read the literature on the psychology of knowledge and action he realized that such a gap was a common phenomenon in many aspects of life—not just in the environmental area, and certainly not just in recycling. He decided to broaden his study to the whole environmental area, using recycling as a case study. We see again the shift from a particular study to a more general one, similar to that discussed above for the Victoria Hill mine site. This required minor adjustment to his research program, and major adjustment to the development of the report.

His major hypothesis, then, was that there was a gap between environmental knowledge and action. His reading of the psychology literature helped him to generate a second hypothesis: that this gap was due to factors that intervened to prevent people from translating knowledge into action. The reading enabled him to categorize these factors under the headings of 'opportunities and constraints', 'social norms', 'personal rewards', and 'perceptions'.

Gerard decided that the most fruitful method of attack was to survey representative people in order to test his two hypotheses. Because of constraints of time and other resources, any surveys he carried out could not be too ambitious. What research instruments would he use?

First, he had to decide how to choose his sample of people to be surveyed (by telephone, mail, knocking on doors, or stopping people on the street or in shopping centres); and what type of survey would be most suitable (questionnaire, focused interview, observation of people's actions etc.). He decided on a 'shopping centre' survey, and chose a questionnaire as his survey instrument. He divided the questions into three parts. The first part asked formal questions about the respondent's recycling actions. The second part was aimed at the identification of intervening factors; the questions were designed to test sub-hypotheses on specific intervening factors. The third part was less formal, with open-ended questions designed to elicit the respondent's own perception of his or her environmental awareness, and the interviewer's assessment of that awareness. This design permitted the researcher to check whether there was a gap between knowledge and action, and to test, by cross checking of answers to the different parts of the questionnaire, which intervening factors were important.

His chapter on 'Method' had one section in which he identified his hypotheses; another section in which he chose surveys as the method to test his hypotheses and justified his choice; another on the choice of questionnaire as survey instrument, including the type of survey; and another on the design of the questionnaire and the reasons for the design. He had to be careful to acknowledge the problems caused by lack of resources (small and possibly unrepresentative samples), and to describe the steps he took to minimize their effects.

I have gone into these two examples in some detail, as it is my experience that the chapter on research design is the one most likely to receive insufficient attention. Although the two projects used quite different methods, the points dealt with are quite similar—clear identification of hypotheses; explicit choice of method; and description of the research instruments to test hypotheses. The research design chapter will then be followed by the 'Results' chapter, where you implement the chosen method and report the outcome.

This sequence may not be suitable if you have decided on a triangulation approach, i.e. you have decided to use two (or even more) methods that are in some way complementary. If you were to describe the design of the research instruments straight after the selection of the methods, as recommended above, your research design chapter would contain the descriptions of two different sets of research instruments, and the next chapter would report the results of the two sets of work. This would disrupt the logic flow. You can overcome this problem in the following way. Stop the 'Research design' chapter at the point where you have selected and briefly described the two methods, and follow with *two* results chapters instead of one. In the first of these results chapters describe the design of the first set of research instruments or procedures using the first method, followed by the application of these instruments and the results obtained. In the next results chapter describe the design of the second set of research instruments, followed by their application and the results obtained. The difference between these two approaches is shown in Figure 5, where only one research method is used (A), and where two methods are used (B). Vineeta Hoon, in her study of the Bhotiyas, had four methods and four results chapters, one on time analysis, one on space

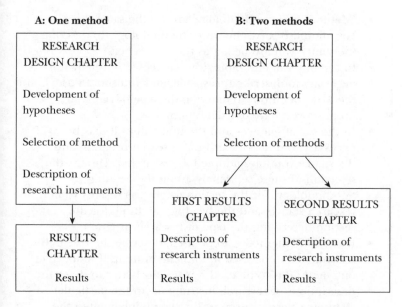

Figure 5: Different arrangement of chapters on design and reporting of your own work for one research method and more than one

analysis, one on energy analysis, and one reporting focused interviews. Each of these chapters included a description of her research procedures before turning to the results obtained.

SUMMARY

- Give the chapter the title 'Research Design' rather than 'Research Method'.
- Draw on the conclusions of the background chapters to identify your research hypotheses or research questions.
- Discuss the range of research methods that could be used to test your hypotheses or answer your questions, and choose the most appropriate method or methods. Don't forget to justify your choice of method.
- If you decide on a case-study approach, justify your reasoning, and justify your choice of case study. Briefly describe the case study. If a long description is needed, say that you will deal with this in a separate following chapter.

- 'Method' and 'methodology' are *not* the same thing. You should reserve the word 'methodology' to describe the stance you are taking as the researcher.
- In the physical and biological sciences it is usually not necessary to describe this stance, and you should use the word 'method' to describe the type of research program you have decided upon.
- In the social sciences and the humanities it may be necessary to describe both the research program and the stance you have adopted as researcher. Discuss the selection of these separately, using the heading 'Methodology' for the section where you discuss your research stance, and the heading 'Method' for the section describing the type of research program.
- If only one method is to be used, describe the research instruments to be used in implementing it. If more than one method is to be used it is usually better to defer the descriptions of research instruments to the particular chapters where you report how you implemented the methods and obtained results.

8 The results chapters

You now have to report the results of your investigations. What should you include in the 'Results' chapter or chapters of your thesis, and what should you leave out? To what extent should you analyse the results and begin to draw conclusions? To provide a framework for answering these questions we shall use the dictum, 'Data is not information, information is not knowledge, and knowledge is not wisdom'.

Data is the outcome of the recording of measurements or images. These data could be recorded by you as the researcher using the research instruments you devised to test your hypotheses, or by someone else on the speculation that they might be useful to somebody, somewhere, sometime. Examples of the second type would be daily maximum temperatures collected at a meteorological station, or the measurements of lead in the blood of children recorded by a public health authority.

When you display the data in a systematic way it may become information; for example it might become clear that the annual average maximum temperatures are tending to increase with time, or the concentrations of lead in children's blood are tending to decrease.

This information may start you thinking. Why is the temperature increasing or the concentration of lead in blood decreasing?

This could lead you to formulate a hypothesis that you may be able to test. For example, you might hypothesize that the concentrations of lead in blood are related to the concentrations of lead in the air breathed by the children, and that this in turn is related to the emission of lead from the combustion of leaded petrol in motor car engines. You could test this hypothesis by plotting the average concentrations of lead in children's blood in particular years against the rate of emission of lead in the same years as calculated from the amount of petrol sold and the concentration of lead in the petrol, as shown in Figure 9 in the Appendix. If you find that the two are significantly correlated you have moved from information to knowledge.

However, knowledge does not become *wisdom* until it is integrated into your whole way of looking at things. It is the implications of the conclusions you draw from your results that become wisdom: new insights, new theory, new paradigms. To be confident that lead in petrol actually causes increases in the lead concentration in blood you would have to build your correlation into a discussion of the whole body of existing work, or even undertake additional work yourself.

This analysis shows us what you should include in the results chapter and what you should leave out. Raw data that does not make sense unless you explain it or display it in a suitable way should be left in the filing cabinet or relegated to appendixes. Data displayed in the form of tables or figures that enable you and the reader to make sense of it becomes information, and should be included. You will be able to draw some general conclusions from an examination of this information. This may go beyond the individual sub-hypotheses that you put forward, to interactions between the variables that you may not have expected and, if you are lucky, to some totally unexpected and quite exciting results.

Both you and the reader now know something that neither of you knew before you carried out your own work. You have stepped out of the information square into the knowledge square. At this point, stop. Keep your theorizing about this for your 'Discussion' chapter, for it is there that you advance from knowledge to wisdom.

Presenting the results

The presentation of your results should *inform* the reader. You may believe that you should include every single figure or every bit of data that you recorded in your work. This is often very difficult because of the sheer mass of data, and is nearly always counterproductive. Consider, for example, Gerard's very modest survey on recycling mentioned in Chapter 7. This included the answers to about 50 questions put to 40 respondents, or 2000 bits of data. Analysis of the results permitted cross-correlations between answers; indeed the method selected depended on examining these cross-correlations. However, had all possible cross-correlations been included, we would have many thousand more bits of data.

Or consider Tony McDonald's work on laser grading mentioned in Chapter 6. This included focused interviews, lasting about one hour each, with three farmers and several professionals in the area of land management. All were tape-recorded and transcripts of them prepared. Should Tony have spent so much time preparing transcripts? (It was all data.) Having prepared them, should he have included them in his research report? If so, where—in this chapter, or relegated to an appendix?

There is a clear set of rules to be followed here:

- Record and file all your data in a systematic way.
- In your report, offer your reader the opportunity of examining these data by private arrangement.
- Include enough of the data in an appendix for the reader to see how you collected it, what form it took, and how you treated it in the process of condensing it for presentation in the results chapter.

For example, Tony in the end included in an appendix the transcript of one focused interview so that the reader could see what relationship the summary of all the interviews appearing in the results chapter bore to individual interviews.

• Present your results in the chapter itself in such a way that it is clear how they relate to the hypotheses.

For example, in his study of the ignition of brown coal particles, Geoff Thomas tested 96 combinations of experimental conditions, with 10 particles tested at each combination, giving results for 960 particles in all—a formidable presentation task. First he averaged the ignition times of the group of 10 particles, and gave the standard deviation to indicate the variability from particle to particle, thus cutting down the entries in the table from 960 to 96.* Although he had performed the experiments in random order, he entered the results in the table in a systematic order. He presented all the results for 1000 micron particles first, then 500 microns and so on. He then arranged the results for each particle size in groups for each of the other variables. The reader could then examine the results with the hypotheses in mind, and develop mental pictures of the effects of the different variables. Geoff could have gone on to plot some of these effects as graphs, but he preferred to wait until the next chapter to do this, because he wished to plot the results against what he would have expected from a theoretical model he had developed earlier in the thesis.

Analysing the results

Having presented the data in an informative way, how much further should you go? In the work I have just quoted, Geoff made some general remarks about his observations before he

---

* If he had tabulated the results for all 960 particles readers would have been so overwhelmed by data that they would have failed to get any information at all.

tabulated the results. The chapter stopped abruptly at the end of the tables. He had a good reason for doing this but, as I look back on the work thirty years later, I find it a bit unsatisfying. He had some strong hypotheses to test. He had designed experiments to test them, and had carried out the experiments. Were the hypotheses upheld or rejected? The reader wants to know what the findings are before the writer goes on to discuss their implications.

In complex situations such as the above, in which there is considerable interplay of the effects of the different variables, it may not be easy to disentangle the results and their implications. Nevertheless, you should try—plot the results in terms of the hypotheses. Geoff could have plotted ignition times (a dependent variable) against the moisture content of the particles (an independent variable), with all other independent variables held constant, or against the size of the particles, or the oxygen content of the gas, or its temperature. He did these plots for his own information, but he decided not to present them as part of the results chapter because he had found that the interpretation of the results was not as straightforward as his original hypotheses indicated. In retrospect I believe the reader would have been in a better position to go on to the discussion chapter had he presented the results as tests of his hypotheses by plotting dependent variables versus independent variables. Then, in a very brief discussion, he could have pointed out the unexpected complexity, and announced that he would be dealing with this in his next chapter.

But don't go to the opposite extreme. I recently examined a thesis in which the candidate had obviously just discovered the power of the Microsoft Excel® chart-drawing facility. His results chapter contained over a hundred charts plotted by trawling through all of his Excel worksheets and plotting every variable against every other possible variable in an effort to analyse the data. His readers were given so much information that they were totally overwhelmed, and learnt nothing about the system that was under examination. Information could not be turned into knowledge. The candidate should have confined himself to plotting charts that tested his hypotheses or that demonstrated something quite striking outside his original thinking.

Drawing conclusions

My dissatisfaction with Geoff's chapter on results was due to its unfinished nature. Hypotheses had been tested, but we did not know what had happened. An aim had been stated at the beginning of the chapter (to report the results of experiments to test hypotheses), but it had been only partially fulfilled.

If you turn back to Chapter 3 in which the structure of chapters is discussed, you will see how important it is that you state the purpose of the chapter in the introduction, and that you write a conclusion in which you describe how that purpose has been fulfilled. This rule is as important for the results chapter as for any other. At the end of the chapter, you should share with your readers your understanding of what is now known that was not known when the chapter began. You will then have transformed information into knowledge.

SUMMARY

- If you have not already described your detailed research procedure in the 'Research Design' chapter you should describe it first before you go on to report any research results.
- You should not include raw, undigested research results in this chapter. Put them in an appendix or back in your filing cabinet.
- Display your results in an informative way, either through charts, tables, diagrams or carefully thought through arguments. In doing so, make sure that the data you have gathered is displayed in such a way that it is possible for the reader to see whether your hypotheses have been tested or your questions answered.

---

9 The discussion or evaluation

Ian Nuberg had reached the discussion chapter of his thesis, and we were talking about how he might shape it. The aim of his PhD project was to determine whether agroforestry could make a worthwhile contribution to the rehabilitation of degraded tropical uplands.* He had spent a year on field research in Sri Lanka, in much the same spirit as Vineeta Hoon's work amongst the Bhotiyas (see Chapter 7), although he at least knew where he would find the degraded tropical uplands. But, like her, he had to adapt his research methods to accord with what he found around him.

In the end, he carried out two major research programs: a comparative study of existing land uses, and an economic analysis of a particular agroforestry system sponsored by a German aid agency. He had written chapters of his thesis describing the results of these studies, as well as the appropriate background chapters, but now found himself in trouble trying to pull it all together. I asked him whether he knew what the overall

---

* Agroforestry is the integration of tree crops, annual crops and/or animal production in the one farming system so as to benefit from the ecological and economic interaction between them.

conclusions of his research project were. 'More or less', he replied. 'Enough to write them all down?' 'Yes'.

When you have analysed the results of your experiments or surveys you are much more knowledgeable than when you started your project, but you have not yet done any real research. You now have to establish what can be concluded from these results. This is where you can advance from knowledge to wisdom, where you might be able to establish new theories or new ways of looking at things. This is the task of the discussion chapter. Once Ian realized that he knew what he had concluded (more or less!), the task of writing the discussion that enabled him to get to these conclusions suddenly seemed less formidable.

Shortly, we shall suggest a method for tackling the discussion chapter that turns it into a relatively easy chapter to write, rather than the most difficult. For a few years now we have been encouraging our students to use this method, and it has worked for them.*

The task of the chapter

Why does the discussion chapter worry students so much? The reason appears to be a variation on the problem we tackled in Chapter 3, that of the tension between the creative and the rational parts of our brains. In the discussion chapter the creative part of our brain is paramount, because we still have to compare the results of our own work with what we might have expected from existing theory to see what new ideas will emerge. Starting to write is, therefore, stepping into the void. Students often try to start their discussion in this way: they thrash around with a hodge-podge of undifferentiated thoughts in their heads, hoping that something will turn up. Yet we know that we must argue the discussion very tightly to convince the reader that the conclusions we draw at the end of the thesis are sustainable. This tension must be resolved.

---

* It worked for Ian Nuberg. See his thesis.

We advocated in Chapter 3 that you resolve this tension by composing a rational framework for the thesis that will get you logically from the aim to the conclusions. Once this framework is in place, you then start to flesh the argument out, giving the creative part of your brain free rein. Your writing might require that you modify the framework, or you might leave it intact and modify the argument. You have set up a fruitful dialectic. We also noted that you could use exactly the same technique when writing individual chapters. Each chapter must have an aim and conclusions, and you must structure the chapter in such a way as to get you logically from the aim to the conclusions. In most chapters it is not too difficult to do this, because you know what the conclusions are before you start to write. However, in this chapter research is still going on. You are still trying to draw out all the implications, so you're not sure what the conclusions are. Therefore you can't design a framework that will enable you to reach them.

Structuring the discussion

How are you to design a framework for the discussion that will enable you to get logically to your conclusions when you don't know what they are? Indeed, if you had *no idea* what the conclusions were, it would not be possible.

The resolution of the paradox is simple—we are asking the wrong question. When we assume that we don't know what the conclusions are, we are only partly right. The rational part of our brain is telling us that we don't know what the conclusions are because it knows that it is the function of the discussion to *find out* what they are. But the creative part of our brain has been working on this problem ever since the research project began. It has been trying out ideas and associations, sometimes accepting, sometimes rejecting, sometimes getting it right, sometimes wrong, but seldom informing the rational part of our brain what it has been doing, or where it has got to. Without this, research would not be possible. We have been doing research in our unconscious, creative minds all the time, and we have reached unconscious, creative conclusions. (Ian knew, more or less, what his conclusions were.)

The key to writing the discussion is for you to bring these unconscious conclusions to the conscious realm, and commit them to screen or paper. Your rational brain can then sort them out and do its best to make sense of them. You can then use them to design a framework for the chapter on the assumption that they *are* the conclusions. This is how to do it:

- Write down all the things that you know now that you didn't know when you started the research, a single sentence for each item. These can be big ideas, little ideas, snippets of knowledge, insights, answers to questions etc. Don't worry whether you are responding to the aim you set yourself in your introductory chapter. That would be a rational approach, whereas you are engaged in a process of dredging up unconscious conclusions. Consider asking your supervisor or a colleague who is familiar with your work to sit down with you while you are listing these conclusions. The presence of another person, chipping in and asking questions, may help you to uncover your hidden thoughts. You will end up with a totally undifferentiated list of twenty or thirty 'conclusions'.

- Sort these into groups of associated ideas (now using your rational brain). You will probably end up with three or four groups. If you have more than four groups, you may have included conclusions that emerged earlier as conclusions to your background chapters, but which have not interacted with your own work. These probably were important at the time, but they are not conclusions from your whole research. You may test this by asking, 'Does this conclusion respond to the aim I stated in my introductory chapter?' Reject those that don't, but first check that you did give them clearly as conclusions in the earlier chapters where they belonged. If you still have more than four groups of conclusions, try coalescing one or more groups to get down to three or four.

- Give a heading to each group. These headings will form the section headings in your discussion chapter. The function of each section is to argue for the conclusions that you will be drawing later. You will have to examine these headings to see which order they should go in. (You will find that some of the groups of conclusions don't make too much sense unless you have already dealt with others.)
- Each section will contain several points, as identified by the separate conclusions that you have already listed for that section. These could form sub-headings within the section. Sort these sub-headings into a logical order, reject ones that are obviously irrelevant, add others that you now see you missed by your earlier haphazard identification process, and coalesce points under one heading if this makes sense (you should not have more than three sub-headings within a section).

You will now have a tentative framework for the discussion chapter. You may now give your creative brain leave to write the text, using this framework. When you start to write, you will not be stepping out into the void.

This balancing of the rational and creative parts of our brains by writing creatively to a rational framework will work only if you treat it as a dialectic. There will be a constant tug-of-war. Often your creative mind will take you away from the rational framework. When this happens, don't assume that the creative mind is always right. Similarly, don't assume that the rational mind is always right. But you cannot leave it unresolved: you must bring either the framework or the wayward text into line. This problem will be particularly acute in this chapter, because the rational framework you are using is tentative, being itself based on conclusions garnered from the creative mind. However, our experience is that at this stage of the research the creative mind has already done marvellous things, and usually you won't have to change the framework much, even though you may modify some of the individual conclusions.

The process we have described probably seems messy, with much experimentation and correction to do. Messy it is, but this is the chapter where research is still going on; it is the only one in which the act of writing might cause you to find out more, where knowledge might become wisdom. Research is a messy process. Nevertheless, you will find it relatively easy to write if you follow the procedure we have just suggested.

Remembering your aim and scope

One function of the discussion chapter is to respond to the aim you set in the introductory chapter. Before they start serious reading of your thesis, most examiners will flip from your introduction to your conclusions to see how your concluding ideas line up with your original ones. They have been asked to do this in the suggested criteria for examination: 'Are conclusions and implications appropriately developed and clearly linked to the nature and content of the research framework and findings?' (See point 5 in Box 2 of Chapter 2.)

The examiners of my thesis criticized me (Paul Gruba) on this very point. I had not linked my discussion section to the overall conceptual framework that I had introduced in my review of current theory. To respond to their criticisms, I had to return to the world of abstract ideas after a long sojourn analysing my own data set. I found that I had to re-read my background chapters, refresh my understanding of their tone and discourse, and re-work my discussion in such a way that I was responding to the major points I had identified earlier. This is not an easy task, but you must place your own study within the larger research framework.

Quite often students find that their work has gone much further than they originally dared to hope, and their original introduction, including their stated aim, now falls short of this. Here is a powerful test for structural integrity that really works. Create a mini-thesis document called 'Logic Check'. Paste your introductory chapter into it. Then paste into it the introductions

and conclusions to every chapter, in order, including the introduction to the discussion chapter you are about to write and
your new and tentative conclusions to the whole thesis. When
you read this mini-thesis through it will be obvious whether
there are logic gaps, repetitions, backtrackings etc. in your
structure. Another version of this test is to write a one-page
summary of every chapter and string them together. Either of
these tests will tell you whether you should rewrite the introductory chapter, including the aim, and also which other
chapters need attention. They will also provide a check on
whether the conclusions you have written really do flow from
your own work.

Writing with authority

By now you have earned the right to comment on the field, and
you can (and must) do so with authority (see the first point in
Box 1 in Chapter 2). How can you demonstrate this authority?
In this chapter you need to address three areas with a critical
eye: current theory, current practice and the conduct of your
own study.

First, you should make sure that you place your thesis within
the theoretical context of the field you are working in. In
addition to making links from the research framework to your
own study, you now have to suggest ways to expand that theoretical point of view. To start, we suggest that you question or
illuminate the accepted definition of potentially controversial
key concepts and phrases. For example Paul suggested in his
thesis that the theorists needed to revise their understanding
of what it means to 'listen' when video is used as a mode of
presentation.

You should also consider existing categorizations of key
factors in your field. Should they be expanded or contracted?
For example, the results of a project on the way refugees access
welfare services in Australia might suggest that we need to
go beyond financial and medical problems to include family

problems. Or the results of a study aimed at developing plans for recycling might indicate that city planners should consider personal and social identity; how they might do this would then need to be discussed. One of your major contributions to the field will be the development and discussion of such factors.

Your review of earlier studies and your own work will also have made you aware of the limitations of current research methods and procedures, and you are now in a position to suggest ways to improve them. What would you do now if you were starting again, and why? Here you can act as a guide for further researchers. Tell the readers which procedures worked well for you, and which did not.

In many theses you will find a section entitled 'limitations of the study'. Whether you put this discussion in a separate section or mention it as it arises, you must deal with it. When writing about the limitations of your own work, don't be apologetic; acknowledge areas that you thought were weak, and deal with them in a straightforward way.

For example, in her thesis on Indigenous Development Projects, Perla Protacio used a nutritional project in the Philippines designed and managed by local people as a case study. In her case-study village, she compared the views of the project held by those who took part in it and those who did not. Her resources were limited, and reaching the non-participants (many of whom lived in inaccessible areas) and communicating with them in the local dialect was difficult, so she was able to interview only fifteen in each group. Statisticians generally think that you cannot get statistically significant results when comparing such small groups. Perla knew this, so she was careful to say what she would have done in an ideal research world, and to acknowledge the limitations imposed on interpreting her results. Examiners will understand that you have worked as an individual researcher with limited time and resources and, if you show that you are aware of the consequences, will not criticize you for 'not doing enough'. However, they will be critical if you do not show that you are aware of such limitations.

116

Another example is the 'case-study' problem mentioned in Chapter 7. In case-study work you have chosen a typical example (or examples) of an activity or a place and are examining it in some detail. Because of the detailed examination you are often able to derive some strong conclusions. But how well might these conclusions apply to other activities or places? This may be difficult to establish, but you must attempt it (Perla spent eighteen pages on this problem). If you omit any discussion of the problems in generalizing from the findings from your case study, you are saying to the examiner one of two things: either that you don't know there are such problems in what a case-study approach is attempting to do, or that you know of them but are not confident of spelling them out.

SUMMARY

Structuring your discussion

- The task of the discussion chapter is to enable you to reach your conclusions.
- You can create a framework for your discussion chapter by drawing up a tentative list of conclusions.
- This can be derived by writing down all the things you know now that you didn't know when you started the project. Rearranging this list under a few headings will give you the titles of the main sections of your discussion.

Checking the logic flow of your thesis

- Before you start writing material in each of these sections check the logic flow of your thesis by stringing together introductions and conclusions for all the chapters into a single document.
- Use this document to check that the thesis, as tentatively structured, enables you to get from the aim and scope you set yourself in your introductory chapter to your tentative conclusions.

Write with authority

- Make sure that your exposition of new theory or ideas places your thesis within the theoretical context of the field you are working in. This will require that you not only draw on your own results, but that you view these against existing theory as expounded in your background chapters.
- Acknowledge any limitations on your findings by referring to limitations of your scope and your research procedures.
- If the thesis involves a case study, check that you have dealt with the problem of generalizing your findings to similar situations.

10 The conclusions

You stated the aim of the research project in your first chapter. The 'Conclusions' must indicate how you fulfilled that aim. They also must arise inescapably from the argument in the discussion chapter. Students often draw conclusions that they had failed to argue for. They had argued for them in their unconscious minds but, because they did not follow a process such as the one we described in the previous chapter for structuring the discussion, they had omitted to back them up in their writing.

It is essential to forge the links between the 'Introduction' and the 'Conclusions', and between the 'Discussion' and the 'Conclusions'. As these are the conclusions to the 'Discussion', it follows that the discussion chapter does not need its own separate conclusions. You could roll these last two chapters into one, giving it the title 'Discussion and Conclusions'. This is often done in papers for learned journals. Alternatively, you could warn the reader in the introduction to the discussion chapter that you will not be drawing formal conclusions to the chapter, but will reserve your conclusions for the last chapter.

Structuring the conclusions

If you followed the suggestion we made in the last chapter you will now have a set of conclusions that emerged out of each section of your discussion, rather than the ones that you originally dredged out of your unconscious mind when you started the procedure. You can now write these down as the conclusions to your research, knowing that you have argued rigorously for all of them, and that you have got them in perspective through your argument. Also, if you put them down in the order in which they emerged in the discussion, they will be in a logical order, because you arranged the discussion in a logical order.

You should now have a deep sense of satisfaction about the whole thesis! Any residual doubts will indicate that something is wrong earlier in the thesis, and you should try to find out what it is. In the next section we provide some diagnostics.

Rules about the conclusions

- We have already hinted at the first rule. If the discussion chapter is where you draw together everything you have done in your whole research project (not just your own experiments or surveys, but also your reviews and analyses of the work of others), then *you should draw your conclusions solely from the discussion chapter.* If you find yourself wishing to include conclusions from earlier chapters that you have not worked over in the discussion, you have either omitted something important from the discussion or, more likely, you are still hankering after more than one aim. That is why we said in the introduction to this chapter that you would be wise to have no conclusions for the discussion chapter other than the conclusions chapter itself.

- *There should be no further discussion in the conclusions chapter.* If you find yourself wanting to engage in further discussion, and even still quoting from the literature, you should have incorporated this material in your discussion chapter (again it is more than likely that you have more than one aim; you have satisfied one of your aims in the discussion, but you still have another aim to deal with).

- *The conclusions should respond to the aim stated in the first chapter.*
  If you take your problem statement and then the aim from
  your 'Introduction', and follow these with your 'Conclusions',
  the result should be a mini-document that reads logically.
  When looking at the first draft of a thesis from one of our
  own students, or examining theses from other students, we
  always put them to this test. It often reveals that the writer
  omitted to state the aim, and it is only when one reads the
  conclusions at the end that one can start to deduce what the
  unstated aim must have been.

- *Summaries are not conclusions.* We drew this distinction in
  Chapter 3 when talking about conclusions to individual
  chapters. It was important there; it is even more important
  here. We will repeat what we said then: summaries are a brief
  account of what you found out; *conclusions are a statement of
  the significance of what you found out*—what you concluded
  from it. If you are merely summarizing the argument developed in your discussion chapter, you will feel quite unhappy
  with your conclusions. There will be no sense of closure.
  Also, you will almost certainly have failed to respond to the
  aim of the whole project. (Sometimes this happens when the
  aim is too modest, or even woolly. For example, when
  researchers say that their aim is to investigate the properties
  of a system, they may end up with a list of properties, a
  summary. This is hardly research.)

- *Conclusions should be crisp and concise.* The conclusions chapter
  may be only two or three pages long—which helps to give the
  sense of closure that we mentioned above.

SUMMARY

The relationship between the discussion and the conclusions

- Your conclusions are what your discussion chapter has
  been arguing for.
- You may write the conclusions to your whole study as
  the last section of a chapter called 'Discussion and

Conclusions' or as a separate chapter called 'Conclusions'.

- If they form a separate chapter there should be no conclusions to the discussion chapter, and you should inform the reader of this in the introduction to your discussion chapter.

Rules about conclusions

- You should draw your conclusions solely from the discussion chapter.
- There should be no further discussion in the conclusions chapter.
- The conclusions should respond to the aim stated in the first chapter.
- Summaries are not conclusions.
- Conclusions should be crisp and concise.

11 Before you finally submit

You have just typed the last full stop of your conclusions. Finished at last! Wrong—you still have several weeks of work to do. You have two major tasks ahead of you: you must revise your first draft in response to the criticisms of supervisors and friends and, when you have done that, you must check the details of the whole work.

- What you have actually finished is your first draft: a collection of chapters written according to the structure you devised. Now you will need to really focus on 'structural editing'. At this point, it may appear to you (and your supervisors) that each chapter is coherent, but you now have to consider whether the whole thesis hangs together. You will also need to check whether your argument really gets you from the aim to the conclusions; whether your aim itself has drifted during the course of the research; whether there is extraneous material that you should transfer to appendixes; and whether important insights have emerged to which you gave little or no prominence in your original structure, but which are now demanding more attention. When you have put all these things right, you will have completed the structural editing.

- As you work through the second draft, you will also need to work on editing details. There are a number of points to check: format, spelling, punctuation, captions to figures and tables, and references. Although these things are not intellectually demanding you have to do them properly, and they take time.

From first to second draft

When postgraduate students have typed that last full stop in their conclusions chapter, they usually print out clean copies of the latest versions of all the chapters straight away, put them in a binder, and give the whole thing to their supervisor to read. Although this gives students a strong sense of completion, and of self-congratulation for all of the hard work they have put in, it is not a good idea. Rather than rushing to the printer, we suggest that you set about revising your first draft *yourself* before giving it to your supervisor. We recommend this not only because it is a unique and necessary experience, but also because the comments that you get back from your supervisor from a document that is in good shape will be more useful than the comments from one that is still full of problems.

What I do with the first draft is parallel to what I expect the examiner of a thesis would do, or what I would do if I were refereeing a paper submitted to a conference or a learned journal. The only difference is that, because I am your supervisor, I am now fairly familiar with the drift of your argument and with the approach you have taken, and I have to guard against reading things into the draft that you have not clearly explained. When you are reading your own work, this is even more of a problem. For that reason, you should put it aside for a few days before you read it as a whole. In this reading you should try to follow the pattern I outline below.

Structural editing

First, I look at the overall structure. There should be a table of contents that corresponds with the chapter titles and main section headings in the text. (If you have reworked some chapters, you may have changed headings and forgotten to change them in the table of contents. If you generate a table of contents from the finished document using the *Insert Index and Tables* command in Word 2000 (see Chapter 4), this cannot occur.)

The table of contents should tell me straight away whether there are any major logic problems. If it is not informative enough, I go to the beginning of each chapter and read the introductions in order. This will probably help, but it may reveal that the introductions themselves are inadequate. If they are, I note this in red ink in the margin of the hard copy.

Finally, I read the introductory chapter *as if I were a reader seeing it for the first time.* I ask myself: Is this telling me (the uninformed reader) why the work is being done? Is it clear what the aim of the work is? Is there an adequate sketch of how the writer intends to achieve this aim? Is the scope of the thesis clearly delineated? Again, if any of these points are inadequate, I note the problems in the margin. Then I go straight to the conclusions, and ask myself whether they respond to the stated aim. If they don't, I note the disparity.

The main text

Next, I read the whole draft from beginning to end, noting spelling, grammar and typographical errors in red ink as I go, and also noting things such as obscurities, patches of purple prose, and places where the argument seems to have logic gaps. At the end of each chapter I write a few lines about how the chapter shaped up in the context of everything that preceded it. The conclusions to the chapter are particularly important here. One of my most common comments on these conclusions is that the author is still writing summaries of the chapter, rather than giving me, the reader, a sense of how the chapter is advancing my comprehension of the argument in the whole document.

By the time I have reached the end, a sense of the integrity (or lack of it) of the whole document has usually built up. If there is a problem, it may be obvious. If it is not obvious, I repeat the first step—the examination of structure—but now with knowledge of how the whole argument has developed (or has failed to). There may be major gaps in the argument; there may be material present that is not part of the argument and that should be relegated to appendixes; there may be repetitions that should be eliminated or consolidated; there may be material that would have been better located elsewhere in the document; there may be conclusions emerging strongly at the end that the author should have emphasized more, or had failed to argue for in the discussion; and so on. Before handing it back to the author, I write a few pages on these larger problems.

Thus the author now has two sets of comments: detailed comments in the text on points of grammar and expression and minor obscurities; and general comments about the structure of the argument. We discuss the latter, and the student gets to work on the second draft. As the student produces revisions of various parts aimed at solving particular problems, we discuss them. I usually find that a complete re-reading of the second draft will not be necessary until after the second, more detailed, part of the finishing process that I am about to describe.

Dotting the 'i's and crossing the 't's

Although the second draft is now essentially complete, you still have a couple of weeks of detailed, rather tedious work to do. Don't skip it—tedious or not, it is essential. The items that you need to check are listed below in the form of a checklist.* We suggest that you photocopy this checklist and actually tick the boxes when you have completed each task. You will see that if you have used your word-processing program to its fullest many of the jobs will already have been done. Also, if you have followed the structural framework we suggested in Chapter 3 and enlarged on in Chapters 5 to 10, you will find that you are just ticking most of the boxes.

Preliminary pages

The first few pages, before the start of your first chapter, are preliminary pages that set the context of the thesis, and help readers to find their way into it. They will include some or all of the following, generally in the order given below:†

Title page

☐ Contains title, author, place, month and year, and the degree for which the thesis is submitted.

☐ Check with your university to see what else needs to be included. For example, the University of Melbourne requires the archive copy of your thesis to be printed on acid-free paper, and this copy must include a notice saying, 'Printed on acid-free paper' on the title page.

☐ Check that the title of the thesis accords with what you have actually done. (There are two dangers here: (a) You may be tempted to use an eye-catching title that could disorient the examiners. This might make you feel pleased with yourself, but it is better to make sure that your thesis passes!

---

* See also, for example, Anderson and Poole, *Thesis and Assignment Writing*, ch. 14.

† You will find more detail on this in any good style manual, such as the *Style Manual for Authors, Editors and Printers*.

(b) You may be still using the title you nominated to the university before you began your project. Almost certainly the thrust of the project will have changed over the course of your candidacy, and you should change your title accordingly. It's a good idea to make the title a cut-down version of your aim.

Dedication

This is optional.

Abstract

This is usually a mandatory requirement for theses.

☐ Have you included it, and does it contain summaries of the three main components of the project, as outlined in Chapter 3, an individual paragraph to each:
— why you did the work and what you were trying to achieve;
— what methods you used and what results you obtained; and
— what you concluded from it.

Table of contents

This sets out the main divisions of the work with the page numbers against them. It is customary to use small Roman numerals for the preliminary pages. Then you start a new list in Arabic numerals for the first page of Chapter 1.

☐ Have you included the preliminary page material that follows the Table of Contents (Acknowledgements, Preface, Abbreviations) in the Table of Contents?
☐ Have you listed all chapter headings and headings of main sections within chapters? (Many authors also list sub-section headings. We suggest you don't—it clutters up the table of contents and robs it of the power to demonstrate the structure of your thesis.)
☐ Have you listed all endmatter (Endnotes if used, References, Appendixes, Glossary)?

☐ As you may have changed things after completing the first draft, check that the page numbers in the Table of Contents are accurate. (If you use the *Insert Table of Contents* command in Word 2000 to generate your table of contents, it is very easy to generate a new one at any time, with the new page numbers automatically inserted.)

☐ Check the styles for table of contents entries set in your word-processing program as default styles, and change them if necessary to make a neater, more informative Table of Contents. It's a good idea to look over several completed theses to see how other students have done this.

List of figures

☐ Check that titles of figures match those in the text, and that page numbers are correct. The best way to do this is to use Word 2000's *Insert Caption* command to generate captions for the figures, then the *Insert Indexes and Tables* command to generate a list of figure captions.

List of tables

☐ As for the List of Figures.

Preface

This should give any information about the preparation of the thesis that you feel to be necessary, for example how you came to embark on the project. Prefaces are seldom necessary for theses. If you do have one, any acknowledgements should appear as part of it.

Acknowledgements

This contains your acknowledgement of help received in the execution of the research and in the preparation of the report or thesis.

☐ Don't forget the body that granted you a scholarship or other financial assistance.

Declaration

☐ This is your certification that the work in the thesis is your original work, and has not been used for the award of any other degree.

☐ If you have published work from your thesis in the learned journals before making a final submission, you must list complete references to such articles in the Declaration or in an Appendix you refer to in the Declaration. You need to do this to avoid possible accusations of 'self-plagiarism' or submitting work that is not entirely original.

☐ Sign the declaration.

The main text

If you have been following the methods we advocated in Chapters 5 to 10, everything appearing in the checklist below should already have been done. But do check. If you have just picked this book up and have not been following our suggestions, we strongly urge you to use this checklist. If you find any of the suggestions puzzling, go back and read the chapter concerned.

Aim and scope

☐ Can the aim be located from the table of contents?

☐ Is the reason for doing the work outlined?

☐ Does the aim follow clearly from this problem statement or rationale?

☐ Are constraints stated that limit the scope of the investigation?

☐ Is the aim followed by a brief outline of the way you intend to go about achieving it? (This refers not only to the experiments, surveys or investigations that you will design yourself, but to the whole of the project, including reviews of theory etc.)

☐ Do the conclusions you draw in the last chapter relate clearly to your aim?

Background

☐ Do the introductions to any background chapters clearly state what their function is?

☐ Is there any material in the background chapters that does not contribute directly to the later development of the report or thesis? (If there is such material, it should be relegated to appendixes, or omitted altogether.)

☐ Do the background chapters justify the formulation of the hypotheses or research questions?

☐ If you are using a case-study approach, does the reason for selecting the case study, and a description of it, appear amongst the background chapters? (It should not, as it is part of your research method, and such material should not be described until you have selected your method.)

Design of own work

☐ Do your hypotheses or research questions spring logically from your reviews of theory and/or practice or your preliminary surveys or experiments?

☐ Do you discuss the possible methods for enabling you to test your hypotheses or answer your questions?

☐ Do you explicitly select a particular method or methods, and justify your selection through your review of possible methods?

☐ Do you explicitly design experiments or other research programs to implement the selected method or methods?

☐ Are tests for your hypotheses or ways of investigating your questions unequivocally built into your research programs?

☐ If you have decided on a case-study approach, have you justified this decision adequately?

☐ Have you justified the selection of your case-study activity or area for its representativeness or typicality or other appropriate criteria?

☐ Does the name of the case study appear in the title and/or aim of your thesis? (It should *not*. If it does, you still have not sorted out the difference between a study of something in its own right, and the use of a case study to develop new theory or ideas.)

Results

☐ Are the results of your experiments or surveys or other own work clearly presented and explained?

☐ Are the major trends or findings identified?

☐ Are you discussing the implications of your results while you are reporting them? (For theses in the humanities areas this might be appropriate, but for theses in the physical, biological or social sciences you should keep them separate.)

Discussion

☐ Do you discuss your own findings in terms of their implications for modifying or extending existing theory or practice?

☐ Does the discussion permit you to reach all of your conclusions?

Conclusions

☐ Are all your conclusions justified by the preceding discussion?

☐ Are you making new discussions while drawing your conclusions? (You should not be.)

☐ Do your conclusions respond to your aim, as set out in your first chapter?

☐ Are your conclusions merely summaries of findings, or do they draw out the implications of your own work for improving theory or practice? (They should.)

Format

You will have to satisfy yourself that the format you have used will help readers to find their way through the thesis and, in particular, that it is consistent. Most books on writing theses give a chapter or more to this, with strict rules about the numbers of spaces before headings, the underlining of major headings, the use of numbering systems, the spaces between paragraphs and so on. These books predate the word processor.

As we argued in Chapter 4, when you use a word processor, an entirely different (and vastly superior) strategy for formatting is open to you—the *document template*. In this strategy, you begin each new document, say a new chapter, on a copy of the template. Then you label each paragraph (this includes headings) with one of the styles predetermined for you in the template. For example, chapter headings would generally be labelled *Heading 1* and section headings *Heading 2*, with normal paragraph text labelled *Normal*. When you have a fully labelled document, go through it, either on the screen or on a hard copy, and check that you have not mislabelled any paragraph. Then ask yourself whether the format for each style is helping you to achieve your desired overall format. If you are unhappy with any particular style (e.g. the style for *Heading 1*), in Word 2000 just select the *Style* command from the *Format* menu and change it, and every paragraph in the whole document labelled with *Heading 1* will be given the new style. You will not have to check for formatting mistakes: the program does all the work for you, and can't make careless mistakes. The only possible mistakes are in your labelling of paragraphs with styles.

Ideally, all of this should have been done long before you got to the first-draft stage. However, even if you have already typed a complete document without using a template, it is still worth doing. Just select your whole document, copy it and paste it into a copy of your template. Then go back over it, labelling every paragraph in it with an appropriate style. This is not as formidable a task as it sounds, because the program by default will have already labelled every paragraph with *Normal* style, and you will have to label only those that are not to remain as normal text, such as headings or block quotations. Once you have done this, you proceed to check, as above, for labelling errors.

☐ When you have a fully labelled document, go through it, either on the screen or on a hard copy, and check that you have not mislabelled any paragraph.

133

Figures and tables

Check all figures and tables. All will have a *caption* that should consist of several parts: a title (which will appear in the lists in the preliminary pages); explanatory material that draws attention to or explains certain features of the figure or table; and a citation giving the source of the material. You may lump all the figures, including graphs (or charts), line drawings, plates, photographs and maps together in one list and the tables in another, although in the past it has been customary to make a separate list of photographic plates (this custom predates the use of colour photocopying and high quality, computer-generated copies of photographs).

All figures and tables

☐ Does the figure or table add an extra dimension to your ability to give a piece of information, demonstrate a trend or get an idea over?

☐ Is it simple or cluttered? Do the important points that you are trying to make emerge clearly?

☐ Does it, together with its caption, make sense by itself, or does the reader have to read the text to make sense of it? (One should not have to.)

☐ Do you draw attention to important points in the caption?

☐ Is there a reference to the figure in the text *before* the figure itself? (A possible exception is photographs that we might loosely call mood pictures. They have relevance in some non-specific way; might not be referred to in the text; and may appear anywhere—although they still need a full caption. Use sparingly!)

☐ Is the title labelled with a standard *Caption* style using the Word 2000 command *Insert Caption*?

☐ Does the title appear in the lists in the preliminary pages? Is the title the same in both places? (If you use *Insert Caption* it will be.)

☐ Have you acknowledged the source or the information on which it is based?

Graphs (or charts)

☐ Does it have both axes clearly labelled?
☐ Do the axes have suppressed zeros? (There are very few cases where this is justified; see the Appendix for our argument on this.)

Tables

☐ Have you arranged it in some way that makes it more than a collection of data? Would the reader see patterns or trends? (There is no justification for putting tables in the text otherwise.)
☐ Have you considered relegating the data contained in it to an appendix, and plotting the main trends as a graph?
☐ Does each entry make a worthwhile contribution to the reader's understanding? (For example, would the reader be able to make a useful distinction between 87.2% and 87.4%, or would it be better to enter both figures as 87%? The additional figures just clutter up the table and make it more difficult to read.)

Notes and references

If you have used the numbered notes system of references, and you have used your word processor to automatically number or renumber notes, you should not have to check that the note numbers correspond to the reference numbers in the text—the program does this for you. It will enable you to collect your notes at the foot of each page or at the end of each chapter or at the end of the main body of text (but collected separately for each chapter), before your 'References'. Give your list a heading 'Notes' (a section-style heading if at the end of each chapter, or a chapter-style heading if at the end of the text).

However, there is still some checking to do:

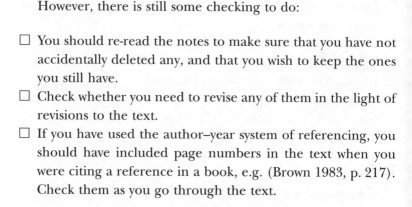

- ☐ You should re-read the notes to make sure that you have not accidentally deleted any, and that you wish to keep the ones you still have.
- ☐ Check whether you need to revise any of them in the light of revisions to the text.
- ☐ If you have used the author–year system of referencing, you should have included page numbers in the text when you were citing a reference in a book, e.g. (Brown 1983, p. 217). Check them as you go through the text.

As you are re-reading your text, check that you have properly acknowledged material taken from the work of others. If it is a direct quote, it must be either in quotation marks or presented as a separate block (see Appendix). The source must be cited, using either the numbered note system or the author–year system. If it is a paraphrase but not a direct quote, you must still cite the source. If you use words or even ideas from the work of others without acknowledging the source you are regarded as having stolen them (the technical name for this is plagiarism). The examiners will probably have read the same literature as you have, and will most likely recognize your plagiarism, and will fail you. Plagiarism is regarded very seriously in the academic world.

Whichever system you use, you should include a full list of sources such as papers in journals or chapters of books that have been cited. The list should be in alphabetical order of authors' surnames, and should contain sufficient detail to enable the reader to find the material in a library. You should check your list for three things:

- ☐ Is your reference list in alphabetical order? (You can use the *Sort* command from the *Table* menu in Word 2000 to ensure this.)

☐ Do the entries conform to an established style?*

☐ Do all the references cited in the text appear in the list? (Quite apart from the inherent importance of this, you will annoy an examiner if you cite material and fail to list it. One way an examiner checks to see whether you know what you are talking about is to check the list of references as you cite them.

☐ Conversely, you shouldn't put references in your list of references *unless* you have cited them. So all of these have to be checked, one by one. Read your own text the way that the examiner would, checking the list every time you come to a citation. (When you are halfway through this, you will wish that you had been far more systematic when you were collecting the reference material in the first place. You'll do better next time!)

☐ You should head this list simply as 'References' in the style of a chapter heading.† This list is often placed after the chapters but before any appendixes, presumably on the grounds that the appendixes really are something tacked on to the end. As the appendixes themselves may have references, there is a case for reversing this order. If you leave the references in the customary place, you should devise some logical method for overcoming this problem, perhaps by having a short list

---

* The order in which the various components are given, and the styles used to distinguish book titles, journal names, etc. varies from discipline to discipline. You should find the method used in your discipline and use it. Departments will often have a prescribed method. If in doubt, consult the *Style Manual for Authors, Editors and Printers*.

† Some people prefer to call it *Bibliography*. A list of references contains only material that is specifically referred to in your thesis, whereas a bibliography may contain other material of interest, but not specifically referred to. For a thesis, *References* is preferable. If you list material that you never cite, the examiners may suspect that you are just padding out your list with material you have never read.

of relevant references at the end of each appendix. Check to see that you have dealt with this problem adequately.

Appendixes

You may have ended up with a rather mixed bag of appendixes after completing your first draft. Some of them will have been written for very good and valid reasons to support material in the text. Others may be leftovers from earlier thinking, and because you were rather attached to them you were loath to throw them out. We suggest some rules for the use of appendixes in the appendix to this book.

☐ Check your appendixes against these rules, and throw out any that are no longer justifiable.

☐ Check the presentation of each appendix that you decide to keep, as follows:
— Does it start on a new page?
— Does it have a title that indicates what it is all about? (Just calling it 'Appendix 3' is not good enough.)
— Is the style used for the title the same as that used for chapter headings?

☐ Is there a preamble that explains briefly what its function is and what it is all about?

☐ Does the preamble refer to part of the main text? If it doesn't, find the part of the text that it supports and make reference to it. If you can't find it, or if the connection is very weak, throw out the appendix altogether.

Glossary

If you have a glossary, it is customarily placed at the end, after all the appendixes. Some writers are tempted to put it up near the front, even in the text itself. Don't do this—it is a special kind of appendix.

SUMMARY

When your supervisor has 'signed off' on every chapter of your thesis you have only finished the first draft of your thesis. You still have two major tasks ahead of you: checking the structure and checking the detail.

From first draft to second draft

* Your first task is to go from the first draft to the second draft. This involves checking the structure of the thesis as a whole.
* Read it through yourself. Check the logic flow. Look for gaps in the logic, repetitions, things in the wrong order. Fix these up as best you can.
* Then (and only then) ask your supervisor to do the same. If possible, find a friend whose opinions you can rely on but who is unfamiliar with your topic to do the same. Fix up the problems they identify.

Checking the details

* You now must check to ensure that you have done everything properly. A checklist is given in this chapter. Photocopy it, and tick the boxes as you complete each check. Depending on how systematic you have been earlier, this task may take several weeks. Allow time for it in your thesis completion schedule.

12 Disseminating your work

This book is about writing theses, and we have emphasized throughout it that you are writing your thesis for a very small readership—your examiners. However, you would not be doing your postgraduate degree unless you thought it was going to lead you into the world of professional investigation, or of research and scholarship. In these worlds you will be writing reports, conference papers, papers for learned journals, and even books.

Doubtless, you intend to publish the results of your project in one of these forms just as soon as you graduate. However, at this point you will probably take employment with some body that has a different agenda from yours, and to establish yourself in your new employment you will have to follow your employer's agenda rather than your own. Our experience is that, as a result, many fine postgraduate projects are never published in any form.

Publishing from your thesis

There are quite a few reasons why you should publish work from your research project:

- Publically funded researchers have an ethical responsibility to make their work available to a wide audience.

- You can use the work from your thesis to advance your career. Whether you intend to pursue an academic position or not, a list of publications will bolster your chances for gaining meaningful employment.
- Publications are a useful way to receive feedback and gain a sense of personal validation.
- Finally, it is simply a thrill to see your name in print: an opportunity not to be missed.

However, if you leave all thoughts of publication of your project for the time after you graduate, the chances are that you will not publish it at all. The way to overcome this is to develop a plan for disseminating material from your project early in your study. The plan should include seminar presentations, conferences and journals, and perhaps even a book proposal.

Preparing a dissemination plan

What is a dissemination plan? Don't be overawed by this. Just think of your work as a series of graded challenges. Figure 6 shows the six challenges that I (Paul Gruba) set myself as I wrote my thesis. This eventually led to actual publications.

Primary	Advanced theory	Pilot study	Central study outcome(s)	New directions related to your central thesis	Spin-offs not directly concerned with your thesis
'Despite use of video in learning ... not used in testing'	'Visual images are open to multiple interpretations; ... comparison methodologies are flawed'	'By investigating four learners, this preliminary framework suggests that ...'	'Upon analysis, a seven-category framework emerged regarding the role of visual media ...'	'There is a lack of media studies in second language contexts ...'	'Earlier thinking that the individual use of computers was best for teaching has given way to a social view ...'

Figure 6: Example of how to convert a thesis into manageable papers

You will notice that you could write the material in the first column in the first year of your work, and material in the second and third columns long before it is finished. Even the overview of your whole project (Column 4) could be written before the thesis is submitted and, as we shall argue shortly, trying to write it will show you very clearly what you have achieved, and will most likely help you to shape your discussion and conclusions.

You should write a seminar presentation or short paper within the first six to twelve months of your candidacy. Most departments will require you to hold your first research seminar within this period. (For example, in the University of Melbourne students are admitted first to probationary candidature and have to hold a seminar as part of the process of having their candidature confirmed at the end of their first full-time year.) Since you have to hold this seminar anyway, we suggest that you turn it into a proper presentation prepared either with over-head projector slides or by using Microsoft Power Point®. It is then a very easy matter to turn this into a short paper that you can submit to a journal that is friendly to students, such as a departmental journal, or perhaps to a conference.

Although we have focused on writing throughout this book, presenting your work at seminars or conferences can also greatly contribute to your chances of passing your PhD. Why? If you make regular presentations, you are likely to sharpen your critical thinking about your topic. The scrutiny your work undergoes in a presentation, both from yourself and from your audience, will help in your writing. To the examiners, it will be clear that you have made an effort to get a range of critical feedback at various stages of your candidacy. Use academic presentations as an opportunity to have your ideas criticized. Of course, you need to do this professionally, and with confidence: remember that one of the examination criteria is that you 'show a command of the area' and 'authority'.

As your thinking matures during the period between finishing your first presentation and revising it for publication, think about writing another journal article or a conference paper, and discuss this with your supervisor. We have called this article 'advanced theory' because it will deal with more complex and subtle points than the previous article. You will find the feedback from reviewers appointed by the conference committee or the editor of the journal particularly useful here. Often, they will detect that it is student work and share insights and make suggestions—which is exactly what you need! Then consider producing another article about every six months and integrate the feedback from them into your thinking about your project.

As you read this you will be thinking, 'It's all right for them, but I have a project to do, and very limited time to do it in. I don't have time to waste on writing papers.' Not so: we guarantee that every hour spent on writing papers will save you at least an hour on writing your thesis, and the act of trying to get a perspective on your own work instead of being continually immersed in it will improve your thesis greatly.

Selecting material for publication

If you are considering publishing as you work, survey sections of your thesis for key points and major challenges. In these early papers you should focus on only one problem (or theme) at a time, and avoid taking on the 'big picture' (leave that for the last paper you write on your thesis). In general, you should prepare such papers with your supervisor as co-author (we shall discuss the problem of joint authorship shortly, including joint authorship with your supervisor). So discuss your ideas for a paper with your supervisor, and develop a plan. This will probably consist of developing a list of section headings together, with you writing a draft to the agreed structure. Your supervisor should then criticize the draft as any co-author would, but in addition you can expect to get some guidance about the 'rules' of paper writing.

Papers for learned journals

We are confining ourselves here to a brief examination of how papers should be structured. Many journals require papers to be presented in a house style, which they outline in a notice to potential contributors at the front or back of every copy of the journal and on their web page. Many journal web pages also contain sample articles for your guidance. If you fail to follow the house style in your submission, at the very least it will delay publication; at the worst it will prevent it.[*]

Structuring your paper

In the thesis you are writing for the examiners, your task is to convince them that you know what you are talking about. In a paper you are reporting material from your thesis, perhaps part or all of one of your chapters, but to a far wider range of people. They are reading it because they are interested in your field, and they assume that you *do* know what you are talking about before they even start reading. Indeed, your paper would not have been published had the reviewers not been convinced of this. You are limited to a few thousand words, and you will have to leave out a lot of material that you included in the original thesis. How should you proceed?

Perhaps you are reporting some experiments or surveys that you carried out as part of your project. In the thesis this material made up one of your 'Results' chapters. You now wish to turn it into a paper.[†] You will need sections on 'Introduction', 'Methods', 'Results' and 'Discussion and Conclusions', although they might not have these titles.

---

[*] An excellent account of all aspects of writing papers is given in David Lindsay, *A Guide to Scientific Writing*.

[†] Further advice on conversion that we've found helpful can be found in the American Psychological Association *Publication Manual*.

In your thesis the introduction to the 'Results' chapter had the task of telling the reader how the chapter fitted into the thesis, whereas in the paper you are introducing the same material as being important in its own right. Therefore, the introduction to the paper will have to cover previous work done by others. In the thesis you had written an extensive review of existing theory in an earlier chapter. You will have to cover this material in the introduction to the paper, but in five hundred words rather than ten thousand! The readers will have to be satisfied with bald statements about this earlier work and your interpretations of it, with enough references for them to be able to follow it up and make their own interpretations if they wish. You then end this introduction with a statement of the aim of the paper. (This is just as important in a paper as in a thesis.)

You now proceed to describe your own work. How much should you include? The usual test is that there must be enough detail for a sceptical reader to be able to repeat it. First, you describe your method, but without spending several thousand words selecting and justifying it. You then report the results, the discussion and the conclusions. In Chapter 8 we recommended that when you report the results of any experiments or surveys you should stop at the point where you had drawn attention to the major trends. All detailed discussion should be set aside for a separate discussion chapter, in which the findings of *all* results chapters would be examined, and implications drawn out to extend or revise the theory in your subject. In the paper you must immediately discuss the implications of your more limited work. In some papers you will see the results and discussion combined in a more or less seamless narrative. This is not easy to do well, and we recommend that, for your first paper at least, you keep them separate. You might also combine the discussion and the conclusions, but if you do this it is easy to 'lose' the conclusions altogether, and again we recommend that you keep them separate.

Preparing papers to be web-friendly

In Chapter 4 we described how to use a thesis template. Using templates is just as important when writing papers, as they permit your paper to be readily converted for web publication. Increasingly, academics are putting their work up on the Internet to be able to share them with other colleagues. By using the template, all of your structural headings (*Heading 1*, for example) will be maintained automatically with HTML. Although many word processors allow you to save your work as a web page, we recommend that you first save it in 'rich text format' and use a specialist converter application such as 'rtftohtml' that is widely available. The extra step will produce a document that is much easier to edit if you need to.

Joint authorship

In your professional life you will write many reports or papers as sole author, but eventually circumstances will push you towards joint authorship. Here we are examining the problem of publication with your supervisor or supervisors, and the even trickier problem of publication of the work of more than one postgraduate project in a single paper.

Writing joint papers is tricky because two or more people are making the decisions. If your joint work is to be really fruitful, you will have to acknowledge these difficulties and deal with them. Researchers who use research students or research assistants to carry out much of their research and contribute to the writing of the paper arising from it, and then fail to make them joint authors, will not do it too often—the supply of assistants or students will mysteriously dry up.

What are the protocols for reporting joint work? Our suggestions, which we will make below, are no more than the commonly accepted rules that permit people to work cordially together. It is far more important to recognize that each of the parties in this joint undertaking will bring to it strengths and weaknesses, and all parties should contribute from their strengths rather than weaknesses. In short, a good professional relationship is far more important than a set of rules. Who is to write what? Who will keep the project moving? Whose name will go first? Who will deal with the editor of the journal?

We suggest the following guidelines. The person who suggests the collaboration should take all the initiatives and be the senior author, i.e. their name comes first in the listing of authors. However, this person should also make the greatest contribution to the thinking and writing. If the initial discussions show that someone else will make the greatest contribution (this doesn't necessarily mean write the most words), then the parties should agree that this other person will make the running and be senior author. If it becomes obvious as the project goes on that the initial agreement about the project is changing, then this should be renegotiated. Don't let it drift!

As we noted earlier, it is a good idea to try to publish papers while you are undertaking your PhD project. But it is a tough game, and for this reason the convention is that you publish such material, either before or after the thesis has been passed, with your supervisor as co-author. This not only acknowledges the contribution made by your supervisors to the development of your research (and to your development as a research worker), but also commits them to a critical contribution to the paper.

For papers reporting the work of students, the student should be senior author. At one time it was common for supervisors to style themselves as senior author in such publications, but this is now less common. Where it still occurs, in our view it indicates a mind-set that sees students not as developing independent research workers, but as research assistants. Of course there will be papers where the supervisor genuinely is the senior author, perhaps having made an advance in thinking as a result of work by more than one student. Even here the supervisor should be scrupulously careful to consult with the students involved, and to acknowledge their contributions appropriately.

Using templates for joint writing

You can easily employ the template method of writing when you are writing joint papers, by arranging for all participants to use the same template from the outset. However, you must decide, fairly early in the project, that one of you will be in charge of 'document control' and be responsible for the master disk and the master document or documents on it. (For papers reporting parts of a student's research project it should be the student.)

Before anyone types a single word, the curator of the master document draws up a template for the master document or documents on the master floppy disk. Each of the partners then selects and names his or her own floppy disk, and the keeper of the master document copies the template to each of these working disks for use on every document opened on them.

Work then proceeds as follows. The partners devise a draft outline, and then negotiate as to who will do preliminary drafts of the various sections. As draft material is produced, each partner prepares printed versions of the individual documents for discussion by the whole team, who make decisions jointly as to what changes need to be made. Alternatively, each member gives any new material to the keeper of the master document, who then pastes it into the master document, as far as possible according to the outline, to produce a draft of the complete report. The team then discusses the printed version of this draft. The keeper will also type in (in bold) problems he or she identified when attempting to fit it all together. The second method is probably more difficult, but may be more fruitful. One advantage is that it generates a new outline, which you can examine using *Outline* view in Word 2000. Perhaps it should not be used until the whole paper is starting to come together.

Whichever way it is done, it is essential that the keeper of the master document be the only one to paste or type new material into it—of course following general agreement from team discussion. The team may develop two or three options for structuring the paper, and incorporate contributions from individual members into these structures in different ways, so long as it is recognized that these are not two versions of the same master document, but rather alternative master documents. Such alternatives should be given quite different names to emphasize their separate status.

Seminar and conference papers

Here you not only have to prepare your paper in a written form, but you also have to talk to it at the seminar or conference. Presenters who read from a typescript, head down, no eye contact, voice droning, with no visual material, soon lose their audience. How do you avoid this? Although you are dealing with the same material, the written and spoken versions should be quite different.

Preparing your paper

Your first seminar presentation is the hardest one. You are certainly not on top of your project yet, but you have to convince your university that the project you are working on is suitable for a PhD study, and that you yourself 'have a PhD in you'. How will you do this?

If you haven't yet written your first draft of your introductory chapter, now is the time to do it, because this will form the first half of your first seminar paper (see Chapter 5). The problem statement tells your readers why you are doing the project. End this with your aim. Follow this with your initial review of the literature. Then indicate what questions arise out of this review, and say that it is your intention to answer them. If you have got far enough you could then indicate the method you propose to use to get these answers. You are unlikely to have got any further than this before your first seminar.

(In later seminars follow the same pattern. Don't assume that you can take for granted that your audience will know what the project is all about. Start all over again with your problem statement and aim. Then follow with background theory, but a much-reduced version of it, because now you want to concentrate on your own work. Still note the questions to be answered, but this time discuss the method you are using to get the answers. Then give a progress report on the results of your own work. In your final seminar before you present your thesis for examination follow the same pattern, starting with the background and aim, but concentrate more on the findings and their implications.)

Conference papers follow a similar format, but the context is quite different. In seminars you are putting emphasis on what you are doing, because you hope to get some valuable feedback from other students and academics who are in your discipline but are not burdened with the detail of following your project. In conferences you are usually presenting a preliminary version of your work, but to a broader audience, often including bureaucrats and professional practitioners as well as academics. You are testing the water: if all goes well you hope later to publish a more mature version of the work in a learned journal.

However, the relative ease of publishing from electronic versions of papers has recently led to a new approach by conference organizers. In many conferences today papers are accepted on the basis of an abstract, and the paper is then printed in the collected conference papers without having been refereed. Those papers that impress the organizing committee will be sent to referees for comment and, following any necessary revisions, will be published in the conference proceedings or in a learned journal associated with the organizers. If the organizers do not send the paper for refereeing or if they have no plan for publishing selected papers, you are free to work it up for publication elsewhere. Thus, the written paper has to make a case for publication, and should therefore be in a form suitable for a learned journal, as discussed earlier.

Talking to your paper

Because one of the intentions of student presentations at seminars is to get critical feedback, you need to talk to your paper in such way that you achieve this aim. This means getting the balance right, and not spending too much time on one part to the detriment of others. Figure 7 shows how you might do this in a seminar. It assumes you have got some results from your own work.

Approximate timeframe (based on a typical 20–minute talk)	Section of presentation	Purpose
Minutes 1–2	Transition/ Introduction	Establish your presence and announce what the work is trying to do. Set a critical tone and focus your work with a concise aim.
Minutes 3–6	Review of current theory	Locate your work historically, geographically and in relation to current theory and practice.
Minutes 7–10	Method and research intruments	Set out how you went about the study, and your reasons for doing so. Put key instruments into a handout or make them available for purview through the web or other available resource.
Minutes 11–16	Results	Present key results, being careful not to overwhelm your audience with too much data. Follow guidelines for effective data presentation.
Minutes 17–20	Discussion and conclusions	Summarize those findings that relate specifically to the aim, note the limitations of your study and suggest ways in which research in this area can be further extended. End, as you began, with an invitation for critical feedback and questions.

Figure 7: A typical plan for talking to a seminar paper

151

The same sort of plan should be followed for a conference presentation, but the balance might be somewhat different, with less time on the literature and more on the results and discussion —but plan it out.

We mentioned above that you should not read your paper. Every conference is blighted by a few authors who insist on presenting their papers by reading the written version. If you are going to read from a typescript it needs to be an entirely different version prepared specifically for reading. Gifted speech-writers can do this, but most of us can't (that's one reason why politicians employ speech writers). A better idea is to use over-head projector slides or Microsoft Power Point slides as talking points. Show the slide and, while it is still visible, talk about what it is telling you and the audience. If you use Power Point you can arrange for a set of notes to be available to you (but not the audience) to remind you of points you want to make. But, again, do not read them—just use them as a set of prompts. (And, while we are on reading, *never* turn to the screen with your back to the audience and read your own slides, word for word. This is an insult to the audience, who want to read it at their own pace and think about it while you are talking about it.)

Preparing your talk using Power Point is a good idea, because this program doesn't allow you to put too much on one slide. If a Power Point projector is not available where you are giving your seminar, use the program to prepare overhead projector slides. Print out black and white copies of the Power Point slides and use these to prepare transparencies for the overhead pro-jector. Power Point produces slides in a horizontal rather than a vertical format, which makes viewing much easier. Your Power Point presentation can also be used to prepare your written paper. Just convert it to Microsoft Word format; this will give you a set of dot points that you can then expand into the written version of your paper.

You can also use Power Point to make handouts, but we've found that it is not particularly helpful to audiences to hand them what is essentially a copy of the slides they have just seen.

We suggest instead that you make a four-page handout and reduce the four pages to present them on a single piece of A4 paper. (In some instances, you may need to expand the handout to 6–8 pages.) On the first page, write out the title and abstract of your talk and all of your contact details, including your e-mail address. End this page with a succinct statement of the problem and the aim of your research. The second page highlights key findings from your critical review of current theory and maps out your theoretical framework. On page three, report the main findings by using summary tables. If you have a particularly complex data set, you may want to show an example of it here. The top half of page four is reserved for a conclusion and the bottom for listing references. On each of the pages have a running header of the seminar or conference name and date, a four-word title of your paper and your name.

Then, from these four pages, use a photocopier to produce a handout on a single piece of A4 paper. To do this, lay down pages one and two on the glass. These pages will occupy a space equivalent to an A3 size of paper. Now, program the photocopier to reduce this A3 size to a single A4 and make a copy. Repeat these steps for pages three and four, and then set the photocopier to produce a double-sided copy of your material. Run off a sufficient number of extra copies and distribute them in advance of your presentation.

SUMMARY

Publishing from your thesis

- Make sure that the good work you have done in your project gets published.
- The only way to ensure this is to have a dissemination plan.
- The plan should be geared to publishing while you are still working on your project.
- Give research seminars regularly. These will give you valuable feedback for your project, and will also form

the basis for conference papers and papers in learned journals.

Papers

- Research papers have a different set of rules and conventions from theses. To publish papers, you will write for a different readership using these different conventions.
- Papers written on the basis of work done as part of your project should in general be written jointly with your supervisor. You will have to work out a way of doing this that respects the input of both parties.

Spoken presentations

- Spoken presentations are entirely different from written presentations of the same material. Never just read your written paper to the audience, or even the same paper with bits left out.
- You could prepare a special written version of it to read, but few people can do this well.
- The best idea is to prepare a presentation using Power Point®, and use the slides as talking points. These can be converted to overhead projector slides if necessary.

Appendix: some notes on writing and presentation

Most books on writing theses deal with the art of writing and presentation. They usually deal also with the conventions that support good expression, namely grammar and punctuation. Our book is not about writing style, but rather about structure and coherence, and we advise you to consult one of these books on good writing. Several of them are listed in the Bibliography.

We cannot deal here with all the errors that we have come across in our reading of draft theses. We recommend that you buy a good style manual, such as the *Style Manual for Authors, Editors and Printers*, and work with it at your elbow. Such books will tell you all you need to know, in fact more than you can take in at first.

Writing style

We all develop a writing style long before we start to write a thesis. Some people can effortlessly write beautiful, clear, direct English that aids communication. Others have writing styles that hinder it: verbose, ungrammatical, turgid, laboured. The strange thing is that such writers seem to be unaware of their faults, and have no desire to improve. It would take another whole book to deal with this; one we would not attempt to write. We suggest that you ask two or three people whose writing ability you respect to do you the favour of telling you what they think of your style (your supervisor may annoy you by doing this without being asked). When they tell you, don't be defensive. Instead, thank them, and think how you might improve it. Most word-processing packages have a grammar-checking routine. Early versions of these were not very smart, and people often refused to use them. The latest ones are much better, and we suggest that you use the grammar check as one of your critics. Try to get rid of those wavy green lines by breaking up sentences or rearranging them.

Thesisese

First, we shall describe one particular style fault, namely *thesisese*, that seems to afflict some students. Such students feel they can best impress the mythical examiners by using a particular form of language. It is easier to recognize the presence of thesisese than to define it. Here are two examples we encountered recently:*

> The assessment will require an analysis and application to the study area of available knowledge about human practices and landscape and weather scenarios influencing fire behaviour and occurrence.

> Implementation targets must be firmly established and the market and political institutional impediments identified and rigorously addressed if meaningful progress is to be made.

---

* Probably the first of these passages means: 'To assess [To assess what?] we will need to know how landscape characteristics, weather conditions and human practices in the study area contribute to the outbreak of fires and influence their behaviour once they have started'. You might try to convert the second passage into simple, direct English yourself. We've tried several times, but have not yet succeeded.

Writers of thesisese nearly always use passive verbs: e.g. 'targets must be firmly established . . . and impediments identified'. If an active verb had been used instead, it would be clear who had to establish the targets and identify the impediments. They like to use nouns derived from verbs instead of the verbs themselves: e.g. 'will require an analysis and application', rather than 'will analyse and apply'. Their sentences are long and complicated. They prefer long and seldom-used words to the short equivalent words common in everyday speech. They love jargon: e.g. 'scenarios', 'political institutional impediments'. You can see why thesisese does *not* impress examiners. You are far more likely to impress examiners by using simple, direct words and sentence constructions. Remember that the university has asked them to look for critical thinking, not obfuscation.

The 95 per cent syndrome

The 95 per cent syndrome, although not exactly a style problem, has a similar effect. Let us explain. As you get further and further into your project, you probably don't realize how expert you are becoming in your area. You don't realize the extent to which you have absorbed the important ideas that have dominated your particular field. When you start writing about your own research, which is about the extension and modification of these ideas, you assume that the reader will be just as familiar with the basic ideas as you are, and you don't bother to go over them. You assume the 95 per cent and concentrate on the 5 per cent.

Wrong! First, very few people in the world will be as familiar as you are with the basic ideas. Who else has spent three years studying them? Second, although your readers, the examiners, may be assumed to be generally familiar with the field of the work, they will not necessarily be familiar with the fine detail of it. Quite often one examiner will be chosen because of familiarity with one aspect of the work, and the other examiner, similarly, because of another aspect. Both will be chosen more for their ability to judge critical thought in the area than for their detailed knowledge. (Our own university, for example, requires that both examiners of PhD theses be attached to or associated with academic institutions.) Critical thought will include clear and critical exposition of existing thought on the topic, rather than taking it for granted and hardly mentioning it.

So, don't ever assume that the examiners will know 95 per cent of what you have learnt during your project, and that you have to discuss only the 5 per cent that you believe is new and challenging.

Use of the passive voice

You will write more clearly if you use the active voice for verbs rather than the passive voice. The grammar check on your word processor will always suggest this. Although it is not always appropriate, you should try. Here is an example (the passive verb is in italics):

> The agricultural reforms *have been seen* to be successful, which has led to a surge in agricultural production and productivity, contributing to higher savings and investment, and the release of large amounts of labour for employment in emerging rural industry, notably town and village enterprises (TVE 1992).

You will notice that it is not clear who saw that the reforms were successful. Even by the end of the sentence it is not clear whether TVE saw that they were successful, or whether they stated that the consequent surge in agricultural production released labour for other activities, or both. Using the active voice forces you to clarify what you are trying to say. In the following version of the same passage we have changed from the passive to the active voice as indicated by the italics:

> Chou and Yung (1991) *showed* that these agricultural reforms had led to increases in both agricultural production and productivity. TVE (1992) *claim* that this increased productivity released labour for emerging rural industry, notably town and village enterprises.

Note that using 'showed' rather than 'have been seen' enables us to avoid using the vague word 'successful', because we now define it, and know exactly who did what. Note also that we have made TVE the subject of the second sentence, rather than just being a reference at the end of it, and so we know who was drawing the conclusion about the effects of increased productivity.

Use of the first person

Over the last hundred years the idea developed that science was impersonal, that the scientist was a disinterested observer of the unfolding of new knowledge. It followed that scientific researchers could not claim any personal credit (or could not even display any excitement) over their discoveries when they came to report them. Theses, reports and scientific papers had to be written in the third person, as if someone else had made the discovery. Every writer knew this was nonsense, and resorted instead to use of the passive voice. So we have the wonderful downhill slide from, *[first person]* 'I observed that . . .', to *[third person]* 'The researcher observed that . . .' (or if this wasn't clear enough, the incorrect, and confusing, 'This researcher [which one?] observed that . . .', or the awkward, 'The present writer observed that . . .'), to *[passive voice]* 'It was observed that . . .' (or, since the use of the passive may prevent us from knowing *who* observed, 'It was observed by the present writer that . . .'). Quite apart from using eight words where three did the job very well, we have manufactured one of the building blocks of thesisese. We have also said something quite false about science.

This tendency has never been as bad in the humanities, where people are allowed to take positions, and the first-person, active voice is permissible and sometimes even encouraged (see the discussion on 'methodology' in chapter 7). Nevertheless, writers in the humanities also often hide behind the anonymous third person.

When writing your thesis, what should you do? Unfortunately, most thesis examiners still belong to the old school. Rima, one of my recent students, decided to use the first person plural in her thesis: '*We* can see that . . .', meaning, '*I* the writer and *you* the reader can see that . . .' I did not discourage her, as I thought it came up well. But one of her examiners didn't like it at all, and grumbled at her use of the 'royal' plural. Perhaps he didn't like being pushed into agreeing with what Rima was saying. Perhaps the use of the first person just bothered him. Fortunately, he was not the kind of examiner to let personal prejudices get in the way of proper appraisal, and he passed the thesis. However, we have come across the other kind of examiner too often to advise students to 'make a statement'. For theses in the experimental and social sciences, we reluctantly counsel caution for a little longer.

However, there are some situations where it is just plain silly to stick to the third person. Examples are given below from two theses in the social sciences that were both dutifully written in the third person, except for the situations listed. Both passed.

- When you are recounting personal experiences:

  I arrived in Sri Lanka in the first week of January 1991. By the end of the third week I had dispensed with the research plan I had brought with me. Seven days of being in Sri Lanka taught me more about the practical circumstances of research there than the seven months of reading had previously.*

- When you are stating personal opinions:

  I would like to stress, however, that I am convinced that what has been written about the Grameen Bank reflects reality in the field.†

---

* Ian Nuberg, Rehabilitating Degraded Tropical Uplands.

- When you are explaining the choices you made in research procedure:

  I am not a native Bicolano so, though I understand the Bicol dialect, I cannot speak it fluently, and people laugh at my funny accent. Though the average village person can understand Tagalog (my own dialect, spoken by the people in Manila), the old and poorest cannot. Moreover, because of lack of use, I had forgotten most of the Bicol terminologies. Thus the Research Assistant was my interpreter.* [Just try putting this into the third person!]

When you are writing papers based on your research project you could be a little more adventurous, as many of the learned journals now let authors use more direct forms of writing, including the first-person singular. If members of the editorial board object, they will soon let you know.

Verb tenses

Some non-English languages don't use tenses, but rely on the context to indicate whether something happened in the past, is happening now, or may happen in the future. In English we have such a rich collection of tenses that we often get them wrong ourselves. This creates problems not only for students whose native language is not English, but also for English-speaking students.

We create these tenses in two ways: by adding endings to the verbs, or by using auxiliary verbs such as the verb *to have, to be, may, will* etc., together with a *participle* derived from the verb.

What tenses should you use in your thesis? Here are some general rules, together with examples (the verb tenses are in italics):

---

* Perla Protacio, Indigenous Development Projects.

- Use the past tense when you are reporting what you or others did at particular times:

  Smith and Jones *reported* the results of their investigation of housing trends in their book published in 1985.

- Use the perfect tense when you are reporting what you or others did in the past, but not at specific times:

  Because of their great interest I *have reported* the results of these experiments in some detail.

- Use the present tense in an introduction to a chapter or section or a table where you are outlining its contents:

  Section 2.1 *reviews* the state of the housing industry in the USA after World War II.

  Table 3 *shows* that in all countries car ownership increases with GDP per capita.

- Use the present tense when you are discussing the implications of some work of yours or others:

  Smith and Jones reported the results of their investigation of housing trends in their book published in 1985. This work *reveals* that the poorest group in the community find it almost impossible to find adequate housing.

Note that we are changing from the past tense (reported) to the present tense (reveals) in the same paragraph.

- Use the future tense when you are saying what will be done later in the thesis:

  The findings of the case study *will be reported* in Chapters 5 and 6. As *will be seen* in those chapters, the indigenous project did not fare any better than projects designed and managed by expatriates.

Punctuation*

Comma (,)

The comma is the most used (and most misused) punctuation mark. We mention here only the six most common uses, and the two most common misuses. If you are not too sure whether a comma should be used, try reading the sentence out loud. Where you find yourself pausing momentarily, you should probably be using a comma. Where you don't pause, you should probably not be using the comma. Use commas for the following:

- Between a series of items in a sentence, except before the final *and, etc.* and *or*:

    . . . their own surveys, interviews, observations, experiments etc.

Many people think that this exception means that a comma should never be used before the word *and*. This is not so: the rule applies only to the last item *in a series*. An example of when it should be used before the word *and* is given in the next point.

- Between co-ordinate clauses linked by words such as *and, but, or, nor*:

    More recent programs check your spelling for you, and even make suggestions about your grammar.

- To mark the separation of an adverbial phrase or clause from the main clause:

    Before anyone types a single word, the curator of the master document draws up a style sheet.

---

* In the notes on punctuation that follow we are generally following the recommendations of the *Style Manual for Authors, Editors and Printers*, and occasionally paraphrasing entries in it. The examples we give, however, are mostly taken from elsewhere in this book.

- After transitional words such as *however, nevertheless, moreover, therefore, similarly,* and sometimes before them (see *Style Manual*):

    In practice, however, we suggest that you go to the top journals in your field to see how they format published work.

- Between adjectives qualifying the same noun, except before the word *and*:

    Some people can write beautiful, clear, direct English that aids communication.

- To put a word or phrase in parenthesis. (To test whether something should be in parenthesis, try omitting the material between the commas altogether; the sentence will lose some information, but should still make sense.) One comma must be placed before the word or phrase, and one after it:

    This included focused interviews, lasting about one hour each, with three farmers.

Brackets and long dashes can also be used to indicate parentheses (see below).

Common *misuses* of commas:

- Use of only one when creating a parenthesis:

    This included focused interviews lasting about one hour each, with three farmers.

Two or none!

- To mentally 'catch breath' between a long subject and the verb:

    How one could be 'critical' in these circumstances, is quite beyond me.

There should never be a comma between a subject and its verb. Sometimes the subject may be qualified by a phrase or clause in parenthesis, and commas will therefore appear:

The detailed design of the experiments, and hence the physical design of the apparatus, required quite precise hypotheses.

In such cases the 'two-or-none' rule applies.

Semicolon (;)

The semicolon is a *separator*, like a comma, but stronger. Its three main uses are:

- To separate parts of a sentence that are too closely related to be broken into separate sentences:

  The story developed surely and clearly; Joe always knew where he was going; and at the end it was completely clear what he had achieved . . .

- To separate clauses that already contain commas:

  An index is located at the end of the work, and will not be read before the work itself; in fact, it is unlikely to be read systematically at all.

- To separate items in a list.

  The three most common types of background chapter are:
  — *Descriptive material* to locate study areas in space, time or culture;
  — *Reviews of existing theory or practice*;
  — *Preliminary investigations or surveys* done by you or others that will help to formulate hypotheses for the major research program to follow.

Colon (:)

The colon should not be confused with the semicolon. They have quite different uses, and cannot be used interchangeably. The three main uses of the colon all have a sense of *introducing* something that is to follow:

- To introduce a list (the various items in the list are then usually separated by semicolons—see example above).
- To introduce something that will amplify or explain what preceded it:

It has only one function: to introduce readers to the thesis.

- To introduce a quotation, although a comma may be used when the quotation consists of one simple sentence only.

Dash, long and short (— –), and hyphen (-)

They are different, and each has its own specific uses. You should find out how to create all three on your word processor.

- The long dash (or em rule) has two principal uses: to indicate an abrupt change in the sentence structure, also to indicate material that is in parenthesis. It should be used for parentheses only when the break is very abrupt. Otherwise, use brackets or commas. As with all parentheses, two or none.
- Whereas the long dash is a separator, the short dash (or en rule) is a linking device. It has two principal uses: to show spans of numbers (e.g. 1980–1990), and to show an association between words that keep separate identities (e.g. human–cosmos relationship).
- The hyphen is used to build up complex words. The most common are words built up from suffixes such as sub- or non- (incidentally, these suffixes should never stand alone as separate words). As time goes on, some of these complex words become words in their own right, and no longer need the hyphen: thus sub-zero, but nonconformist. Consult your dictionary.
- Hyphens are also used to form some compound nouns (e.g. 'grammar-check' but 'word processor') and compound adjectives (e.g. 'light-sensitive'), often from a mixture of adjectives, verbs and nouns. Compound nouns are straightforward—but consult your dictionary to see whether words should be separate, linked by hyphens, or set as one word.

166

Usage varies and is always changing. *Consistency* within any piece of writing is vital.

Compound adjectives can be very tricky. One student came out with 'sulphur reduced residual fuel oil fired brick kiln'. Where should he have put the hyphen(s)? Another produced a 'non-cost of living indexed pension'. The first of these is a mixture of compound adjectives and compound nouns, some of which don't take hyphens (e.g. *brick kiln*). The best solution is to break it up a bit. We suggest *brick kiln fired with sulphur-reduced residual fuel oil*. Similarly, we suggest *pension not indexed for cost of living*.

Brackets ( ) [ ]

Curved brackets (or parentheses), and square brackets have quite separate uses. Don't use them interchangeably. And don't be tempted to use other types of bracket, such as curly brackets (except perhaps in mathematical expressions); no convention exists to indicate their meaning.

- Curved brackets or parentheses are used to enclose expressions that are not essential to the meaning of the sentence but that amplify or clarify or may be considered to be an aside. They are also used to enclose numbers or letters designating items in a list.
- Square brackets are reserved for interpolations. Their principal use is to make your own interpolations inside quotes from other writers. Such interpolations would consist of words you insert to clarify the meaning, or that magic word sic (Latin for 'thus') to indicate that the original author, not you, was responsible for an obvious misspelling or inaccuracy.

Quotation marks ('. . .' ". . .")

The principal use of quotation marks is to enclose the *exact* words of a writer or speaker, whether or not these form a complete sentence or sentences. Use *single* quotation marks. Use double quotation marks *only* for quotations within quotations.

There are other ways of indicating quotations, and other uses of quotation marks. These are the principal ones:

- Long quotes from the work of others, say longer than fifty words, should not be designated by quotation marks and contained within the normal text, but should be presented as a separate block. The whole block should be in slightly smaller type, indented, with space above and below. Quotation marks are not needed, and should not be used. And the quote should not be in italics.

- Quotation marks (again, single marks) are used to indicate that the enclosed words are the title of a chapter in a book, a paper in a journal, a poem etc.

- Quotation marks are also used to indicate colloquial words in formal writing, or technical words in non-technical writing. After the first use of the word the quotation marks may be omitted. Many writers extend this use by putting pet words or humorous expressions in quotes. It is best to avoid this as much as possible: it can become a bad habit.

Words

Link words

We use link words to indicate the logic flow in a passage of text. They are of two kinds: *conjunctions,* which are used inside sentences to link clauses, and *transitional words,* which are used to link a sentence to the one that preceded it. Many writers seem to use them interchangeably. This is a great source of confusion.

Conjunctions are used to link an adverbial clause in a sentence to the main clause. The adverbial clause defines the time, place, manner, or cause of the main action. They are also used to link co-ordinate clauses in a sentence; such clauses are related to each other, but one does not define the other in any way. Commonly used conjunctions are: *but, although, unless, if, as, since, while, when, before, after, where, because, for, whereas, and, or, nor.* If you are in doubt as to whether a word is a conjunction, and can therefore be used to link two clauses in the same sentence, check your dictionary. Conjunctions will have the abbreviation *conj.* after them.

In each of the following sentences the conjunction is placed in italics:

> In the discussion chapter the creative part of our brain is paramount, *because* this is the part of the thesis where we are still doing research.

> *If* you are to become a participant, you will need to have some practical experience of your own.

> *When* you have finished writing for the day, save what you have written.

> *Since* this happened I have asked students to include all the preliminary pages when they submit their second drafts.

> You will have two themes bumping along in your report together, *and* the reader will not be able to work out what you are doing.

Whereas conjunctions are used to link clauses within a sentence, transitional words are used to link one sentence to the next. Commonly used transitional words are: *however, thus, therefore, instead, also, so, moreover, indeed, furthermore, now, nevertheless, likewise, similarly, accordingly, consequently, finally.* Some transitional phrases are also available: *in fact, in spite of, as a result of, for example, for instance.* A conjunction cannot be used to begin a single main clause; a transitional word always can. A conjunction cannot be separated from its clause by a comma; a transitional word can. Transitional words appear in the dictionary as adverbs: if you cannot find the abbreviation *adv.* after a word, then don't use it as a transitional word. (The words *but* and *or* are shown in the dictionary as both conjunctions and adverbs, and can be used as transitional words. The words *for* and *and* are only conjunctions, but are occasionally allowed to break the rule in very special cases, and appear as transitional words. There are no other exceptions.)

In the following sentences the transitional words are shown in italics. You will notice that each of the sentences consists of a single clause:

Thus we see that research is a peculiar mixture of creative thinking and rational thinking.

You have to be a bit careful of the word 'method', *however*.

But this was not her problem.

So, let me ask another question.

Finally, you will report on the specific design of the investigation.

And why might the attempt be beneficial?

The first six of the transitional words on the list are commonly *misused* as conjunctions, as shown in the following:

In such reports the underlying theory used as a framework for the investigation might be reviewed *however* it is unlikely that new or improved theory would be developed.

You will have two themes bumping along in your report together, *therefore* the reader will not be able to work out what you are doing.

The opposite fault is also not uncommon—conjunctions used as transitional words:

Although this was not her problem.

Whereas this is the part of the thesis where we are still doing research.

Repair Words

In spoken language we often use what we might call 'repair' words to patch up sentences that are going wrong. We can get away with a lot in spoken language, because the audience can hear the tone of our voice and the pauses while we struggle for the right way of saying what we mean. But in the written word it just results in a mess. Here is a list of the most common repair words:

regard (as in 'as regards' or 'in regard to')
terms (as in 'in terms of'—this has recently become very popular)
aspect
issue (this is everyone's favorite repair word)
relation (as in 'in relation to')
compared with or *to* ('if we consider elephants we find that they are large compared to lions' rather than 'elephants are larger than lions')
address, embrace and *resolve* (usually 'issues' get these)
relative to
former and *latter*
basically

We're not suggesting that these are not legitimate words, but rather that you should not use them to fudge things when you can't really work out what you are trying to say. 'Authoritative' people often use these words, perhaps because fudging is sometimes advantageous and it becomes a habit of mind, but in theses it just doesn't work. Take, for example, the sentence, 'One issue that has to be resolved is the issue of housing for low-income people'. The writer is trying to hint that there is some problem with housing for this group, perhaps price, perhaps availability, perhaps the whole political system that makes it nearly impossible for them to get decent houses. Unfortunately, it says nothing clearly.

Run the *Find* command from the *Edit* menu in Word 2000 over your work to find the offending word or words, and reconstruct the sentences to get rid of as many of them as you can. For some words such as *in terms of* or *with regard to* reconstruction may be quite simple: reversing the sentence order, or changing from passive voice to active voice. But for that word *issue* you will have to take the time to say what you really want to say. Often you will need two or three sentences to do this. Using the word *issue* is just a way of avoiding the labour of stating clearly what you want to say.

Frequently misused words

These are words that have a strict definition, which is then used in a metaphorical sense related to their original meaning. Here are a few favourite ones, but there are many others: *parameter; focus; scenario; viable; empowerment; highlight; core; explore; stem; mainstream; significant; key; ramifications; aspect; facet; huge; immense.*

There is nothing wrong with these words, but if you use them metaphorically, you must use them in a way that is consistent with their original meaning. A good dictionary will usually give this metaphorical meaning also. Take, for example, *highlight.* The dictionary meaning (Webster) is 'the lightest spot or area in a painting'. The metaphorical meaning is 'an event or detail of major significance'. Use it only in this second sense. Another example is *viable.* The dictionary meaning is 'capable of living'. The metaphorical meaning is 'capable of existence and development as an independent unit'. Don't stray beyond this second meaning. When in doubt, look up the dictionary!

Figures and tables

What is the function of graphs, diagrams and photographs? Why are you using them? The immediate answer to this question is always: 'I use them when they express the point I wish to make more clearly than the written word does'. Although this is usually true, we believe it is only part of the truth. If you wish to get the best out of your graphic material, it is necessary to put yourself in the position of the reader.

How do readers use graphic material? Do they read the written text until they get to the sentence, 'Figure 6.2 shows that increasing the population density decreases the per capita consumption of petrol', and then dutifully find Figure 6.2 to check that this is indeed so? Our experience is that long before readers begin Chapter 6 they will have opened the thesis and skimmed through it, 'reading' the diagrams and looking at the photographs. This will trigger certain thought processes and tentatively implant certain images. There may be other preliminaries, such as looking for the aim of the research and reading the conclusions. Then the real reading begins. The written text develops ideas in the way that the writer intended, and readers will no doubt follow these ideas. But at the same time they will be generating their own set of ideas. They will compare written text in one chapter with diagrams or text in another in ways that the writer had not intended. They might refer to and puzzle over Figure 6.2 long before the writer draws attention to it. They might return to it again when something written in Chapter 8 triggers another thought. If you reflect on it, you will probably realize that you read things in a similar way yourself.

Readers use several complementary channels of communication simultaneously, some using words and some using visual images. (Other media such as theatre or television use sound channels also.) Readers do not use one at a time, switching from one to the other. Rather they use all of them simultaneously, perhaps giving one more attention than others at any given moment. Think of lectures you have been to where the lecturer has used overhead-projector slides to complement the spoken word. You are busy looking at one of the slides and thinking about it, while still listening to what is being said, when suddenly, much to your annoyance, the slide disappears. The lecturer, already busy with the next point, didn't think it was of any more interest to you, but *you* were busy integrating it with the rest of what was going on in the lecture.

This leads us to some rules about visual material:

- Although a figure or table will nearly always be 'called up' by the written text, the reader should not have to read that part of the text to make sense of it. It should make sense by itself. You should fully explain the context in the caption, and draw attention to features you wish the reader to note, even if you have discussed these in some detail in the text.

- Try not to cram in too much detail. When we ask students their view on the functions of tables they often reply that it is to record data such as experimental readings in a systematic way. This being so, they argue, a table might have to contain large amounts of data, perhaps extending over several pages, and with each entry given to four or five significant figures. Such data should not go in the main text, but rather in an appendix. A table in the main text must be a complementary channel of communication, and large masses of undigested data will never be that. You should put a table in the main text only when the patterning obtained by arranging things in rows and columns will tell the reader something better than or different from a normal written description. If the data in your table seems to you to demonstrate some trend or correlation, you should consider displaying the trend by means of a graph in the main text, and banishing the figures to a table in an appendix.

- When demonstrating trends or correlations in a graph, think carefully about what you are trying to demonstrate. Usually you will be either confirming an established model or developing a new one, and you should have this in mind when plotting your graph. Authors often suppress the zero point on one or both of the axes 'to make best use of the available space', or so students frequently say. Apparently this is part of the folklore of 'graphs' learnt at school. Forget it! It is far more important to think about the trends or correlations you are trying to demonstrate than to enable someone to scale off values from your graph with great accuracy.*

A similar error is the introduction of an extraneous variable. You will often see this in newspapers, where the journalist is

---

* This is our only point of disagreement with the *Style Manual for Authors, Editors and Printers*. Its argument seems to be based on graphs being 'visually effective'. We base our argument, rather, on whether they are effective at demonstrating the point in question.

trying to demonstrate a relationship between two variables that are both changing with time. Figure 8 is a striking example of this. The authors were trying to demonstrate that reducing the lead emissions into urban air from the combustion of petrol that contained lead would reduce the lead concentration in the blood of children. The data available to them were figures taken in the USA over the five-year period 1976–80. The lead emissions had been dropping over the period, apparently in response to progressive reductions in the lead content of petrol. The writers plotted both the quantity of lead in petrol sold in major cities and the lead content of the blood of children in those cities against time in years. They suppressed the zero on both axes, and chose the scales in such a way that the two curves followed each other almost exactly, as shown in Figure 8, which has been reproduced from their work.

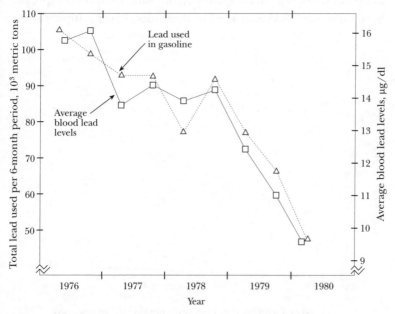

Figure 8: Lead emitted from burning petrol, and level of lead in children's blood, 1976–1980

SOURCE: Committee on Advances in Assessing Human Exposure to Airborne Pollutants in *Human Exposure Assessment for Airborne Pollutants: Advances and Opportunities,* National Academy Press, Washington, 1990, p. 230.

In this graph the year in which the measurements were taken is introduced as an extraneous variable, and the zero is suppressed for both variables. The obvious (but wrong) conclusion that the unwary reader would draw from it is that lead in blood is proportional to lead from burning petrol, with the corollary that all that one has to worry about in a program to control lead in blood is reducing the lead emissions from burning petrol. If the authors had plotted one against the other, without worrying about the distraction of the years in which the various values were generated, and had refrained from suppressing the zeros, they would have found the correlation shown in Figure 9.

Clearly, lead from petrol *is* strongly correlated with lead in children's blood, as the authors of Figure 8 had presumed. However, projecting the correlation line down to the y-axis shows that some other factor must be involved also. Even if lead were to be eliminated entirely from petrol, some children might still have quite high levels of lead in their blood from other causes.

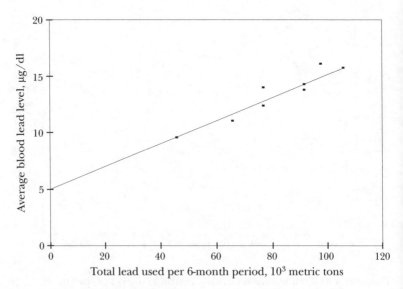

Figure 9: The relationship between lead emitted from burning petrol and the level of lead in children's blood

Appendixes

Appendixes or annexes, as we can tell from the derivation of the two words, are things appended to or tacked on to the main text of a report or thesis. They do not contribute to the main argument, but have been included to support it in some way. They might establish the context of an item in the main text, or give the derivation of an equation. They are often used as a repository for raw data. They might give a sample of a completed questionnaire (in this case the main text would describe how the researcher constructed and administered the questionnaire, and would summarize the results obtained).

How do you decide what you should include in the main text, and what you should relegate to appendixes? In the University of Melbourne PhD candidates are given a word limit: theses must not exceed 100 000 words, exclusive of appendixes. Students often find that they have exceeded this limit, and the typical reaction is, 'Well, I'll have to put something in an appendix'. Although this sounds a bit arbitrary, it does make sense. The university is saying that if your argument takes more than a hundred thousand words, it is too diffuse, and probably you have included material that you *should* put into appendixes. But what should go? The test is quite simple: any material that would distract the reader from the argument proceeding in the main text should not be there, no matter how interesting it is, or how essential that the reader have access to it. An obvious example is the inclusion of detailed references to enable the reader to follow up material quoted from other works. It is essential that references be included in the report or thesis, but it is obvious that quoting the detail of them in the middle of the main text would be quite distracting. A list of references at the end of the report is a type of appendix. However, this is a test for *excluding* material from the main text, not for including it in an appendix. It might be that you should exclude it from your thesis altogether.

We need another test to decide what to *include* in appendixes. Robert gave me a draft chapter of his thesis to read, and it was obvious to me that, although he had put some of the material in an appendix, much of what he had left in the main text failed the first test—it interrupted the flow of his argument. I sent him off to apply this test for himself. In his revised version, with the superfluous material relegated to an appendix, the argument in the text flowed nicely. But to my astonishment I found that one of the appendixes itself had an appendix—the original appendix was now tacked on as an appendix to material that was itself now relegated to an appendix. He had written it, and couldn't let it go. Finally, perhaps to humour me, he omitted it altogether (no one missed it). Don't include material in appendixes unless you are fairly sure that it is necessary to support your argument. If it is a thesis, try to imagine yourself in the examiner's place and ask, 'Would I want to follow this up?' This is not a very strong test, but it is worth applying.

As appendixes are there to support material in the main text, you should insert a reference to them at the appropriate point in the main text. Don't include appendixes that you do not refer to in the text. (You may think that this is too obvious to mention, but we can assure you that we have often seen stand-alone appendixes.) Nevertheless, you should give the appendix an appropriate title (not just 'Appendix 3', but 'Appendix 3: Derivation of the logistic equation'), and should briefly explain its function.

Bibliography

American Psychological Association, *Publication Manual of the American Psychological Association*, 5th edn, American Psychological Association, Washington DC, 2001.

Anderson, J. & Poole, M., *Thesis and Assignment Writing*, 2nd edn, John Wiley & Sons, Brisbane, 1994.

Arnold, J., Poston, C. & Witek, K., *Research Writing in the Information Age*, Allyn & Bacon, Boston, 1999.

Belsey, C., *Critical Practice*, Methuen, London, 1980.

Committee on Advances in Assessing Human Exposure to Airborne Pollutants, *Human Exposure Assessment for Airborne Pollutants: Advances and Opportunities*, National Academy Press, Washington DC, 1990.

Day, A., *How to Get Research Published in Journals*, Gower, Aldershot, UK, 1996.

Denzin, N. K. & Lincoln, Y. S. (eds) *Handbook of Qualitative Research*, Sage, Thousand Oaks, Calif., 1994.

Fink, A., *Conducting Research Literature Reviews*, Sage, Thousand Oaks, Calif., 1998.

Fitzpatrick, J., Secrist, J. & Wright, D. J., *Secrets for a Successful Dissertation*, Sage, Thousand Oaks, Calif., 1998.

Girden, E. R., *Evaluating Research Articles: From Start to Finish*, Sage, Thousand Oaks, Calif., 1996.

Glatthorn, A. A., *Writing the Winning Dissertation: A Step-by-step Guide*, Corwin Press, Thousand Oaks, Calif., 1998.

Goodlad, S., *Speaking Technically: A Handbook for Scientists, Engineers, and Physicians on How to Improve Technical Presentations*, Imperial College Press, London, 1996.

Holt, G. D., *A Guide to Successful Dissertation Study for Students of the Built Environment*, Built Environment Research Unit, University of Wolverhampton, Wolverhampton, UK, 1998.

Hoon, V., *Living on the Move*, Sage Publications India, New Delhi, 1996.

Hult, C. A., *Researching and Writing in the Social Sciences*, Allyn and Bacon, Boston, 1996.

Koestler, A., *The Sleepwalkers*, Penguin, Harmondsworth, UK, 1959.

Lewins, F. W., *Writing a Thesis: A Guide to its Nature and Organization*, Bibliotech, Canberra, 1993.

Lindsay, D., *A Guide to Scientific Writing*, Longman Cheshire, Melbourne, 1984.

McLean, P. *Surviving a Research Thesis: A Discussion of Issues Relating to Time Management, Motivation and Supervision*, Learning Skills Unit, University of Melbourne, 1994.

Miles, M. B. & Huberman, A. M., *Qualitative Data Analysis: An Expanded Sourcebook*, Sage Publications, Thousand Oaks, Calif., 1994.

Murrell, G., Huang, C., & Ellis, H., *Research in Medicine: Working towards a Thesis in the Medical Sciences*, Cambridge University Press, Cambridge, 1999.

Orna, E., *Managing Information for Research*, Open University Press, Buckingham, UK, 1995.

Phelan, P. & Reynolds, P., *Argument and Evidence: Critical Analysis for the Social Sciences*, Routledge, New York, 1996.

Preece, R. A., *Starting Research: An Introduction to Academic Research and Dissertation Writing*, Pinter Publishers, New York, 1994.

Reynolds, L. & Simmonds, D., *Presentation of Data in Science*, Martinus Nijhoff Publishers, The Hague, 1983.

Rountree, K. & Laing, T., *Writing by Degrees: A Practical Guide to Writing Theses and Research Papers*, Longman, Auckland, 1996.

Rudestam, K. E., & Newton, R. R., *Surviving Your Dissertation: A Comprehensive Guide to Content and Process*, Sage, Newbury Park, Calif., 1992.

Sides, C. H., *How to Write and Present Technical Information*, Cambridge University Press, Cambridge, 1992.

Silverman, F. J., *Authoring Books and Materials for Students, Academics and Professionals*, Praeger, Westport, Conn., 1998.

Sprent, P., *Getting into Print: A Guide for Scientists and Technologists*, E&FN Spon, London, 1995.

Style Manual for Authors, Editors and Printers, 6th edn, John Wiley (formerly Australian Government Publishing Service), Australia, 2002.

Teitelbaum, H., *How to Write a Thesis: A Guide to the Research Paper*, Macmillan, New York, 1994.

Thomas, Shane, *How to Write Health Sciences Papers, Dissertations and Theses*, Harcourt Publishers, Edinburgh, 2000.

Turner, G. W. (ed.), *Australian Concise Oxford Dictionary*, Oxford University Press, Melbourne, 1987.

University of Melbourne, *The Degree of Doctor of Philosophy Handbook*, School of Graduate Studies, University of Melbourne, 2000.

Whimster, W. F., *Biomedical Research: How to Plan, Publish, and Present it*, Springer, Berlin, 1997.

Yin, R. K., *Case Study Research: Design and Methods*, Sage, London, 1994.

Zerubavel, E., *The Clockwork Muse: A Practical Guide to Writing Theses, Dissertations, and Books*, Harvard University Press, Cambridge, Mass., 1999.

Zobel, J., *Writing for Computer Science: The Art of Effective Communication*, Springer, New York, 1997.

http://www.ndltd.org/members/index.htm

Theses referred to

Gruba, P., The Role of Digital Video Media in Second Language Listening Comprehension, PhD, University of Melbourne, 1999.

Hanson, G., Recycling Policy in Australia, MEnvS, University of Melbourne, 1997.

Hoon, V., Himalayan Transhumance and Nomadism, PhD, University of Madras, 1989.

Ives, M. J., The Human Relationship to Agricultural Land, PhD, University of Melbourne, 1999.

Jarayabhand, S., Management of Coastal Aquaculture in Thailand, PhD, University of Melbourne, 1997.

McDonald, A., Long and Short Term Effects of Laser Grading upon Irrigated Agricultural Land in Victoria, MLArch Research Report, University of Melbourne, 1989.

Mutimer, G., Environmental Attitudes and Behaviour, BPD (Hons) Research Report, University of Melbourne, 1991.

Nuberg, I. K., Appropriate Interventions for Rehabilitating Degraded Tropical Uplands, PhD, University of Melbourne, 1993.

Protacio, P. M., Indigenous Development Projects, PhD, University of Melbourne, 2000.

Schapper, J. A., Criteria for the Assessment of Landscape as Heritage, PhD, University of Melbourne, 1994.

Sivam, A., An Approach to Improved Housing Delivery in Large Cities of Less Developed Countries, PhD, University of Melbourne, 1999.

Sutiprapa, J., Equitable and Sustainable Development in Less Developed Countries, PhD, University of Melbourne, 1997.

Thomas, G. R., Ignition of Brown Coal Particles, MEngSc, University of Melbourne, 1970.

Wakeham, E., The Mining Heritage Landscape: Our Cultural Past, Present and Future, BPD (Hons) Research Report, University of Melbourne, 1992.

Index